STEF SOTO, TACO QUEEN

STEF SOTO,
TACO QUEEN

By Jennifer Torres

For product information and technology assistance, contact us at Customer & Sales Support, 888-915-3276

National Geographic Learning | Cengage
1 Lower Ragsdale Drive
Building 1, Suite 200
Monterey, CA 93940

National Geographic Learning, a Cengage company, is a provider of quality core and supplemental educational materials for the PreK–12, adult education, and ELT markets. Cengage is a leading provider of customized learning solutions with employees residing in nearly 40 different countries and sales in more than 125 countries around the world. Find your local representative at **NGL.Cengage.com/RepFinder**.

Visit National Geographic Learning online at **NGL.Cengage.com/school**

ISBN: 978-0-3571-0648-8

Printed in Mexico

Print Number: 02   Print Year: 2021

For my parents, Lorraine and Sam Torres

CHAPTER
1

Papi had pretty much promised to stop bringing Tía Perla to Saint Scholastica School, but when the last bell rings on a Monday afternoon, there she is just the same, waiting for me in the parking lot: Tía Perla, yet again. Tía Perla, like always. Tía Perla, huffing and wheezing and looking a little bit grubby no matter how clean she actually is. Tía Perla, leaving anyone who comes near her smelling like jalapeños and cooking oil, a not-exactly-bad combination that clings to your hair and crawls under your fingernails. Tía Perla, Papi's taco truck, stuffed into a parking space meant for a much smaller car. A normal car. A station wagon! Something beige or black or white, with four doors and power windows.

I must look as annoyed as I feel because just then, my best friend, Amanda Garcia, stops explaining how she turned an old T-shirt into a new headband and wags her finger. "Watch it, Stef," she warns in her best scolding-abuelita voice. "Keep rolling your eyes like that, and they'll get stuck up there."

I roll my eyes at her so hard they almost bounce off my forehead. She snorts, pulls the headband over her ears, and jogs off to soccer practice, leaving me to deal with Papi and old Tía Perla on my own.

I didn't mind the taco truck when I was younger, and seeing Tía Perla in the parking lot of my Catholic school meant corn chips and cold soda for all my friends. Back then, when Papi lifted me up into her front seat, I was playground royalty. No one *else* got picked up in a taco truck.

But now hardly anyone else gets picked up *at all*, let alone in a taco truck.

I've been negotiating for months, trying to persuade Mami and Papi to let me walk alone—not even all the way home, just to the gas station a few blocks away from Saint Scholastica where Papi parks the truck most afternoons. I'd head straight there, I swore. Wouldn't stop for anything; wouldn't talk to anybody. I could tell they weren't crazy about the idea, but this weekend, Mami and Papi had finally given in.

So why was Tía Perla in the parking lot, with Papi in the front seat, waving?

I drop to the ground, pretending to tie my shoelace and thinking, Maybe if I'm down here long enough, Papi will remember our agreement, *leave*, and meet me at the gas station like we planned.

Instead, he honks the horn and waves even more wildly.

"Uh, isn't that your dad, Estefania?" Julia Sandoval asks, louder than she really needs to.

Just perfect. I stand up and gush, "Thank you, Julia. *So* much. You are *always. So. Helpful.*"

She just tilts her head and flashes her sparkling-sweet smile.

I walk across the parking lot, eyes glued to the ground and arms crossed sourly against my chest. I don't look up—not even when I'm climbing into the truck—until Papi asks, like he asks every single day, "Aprendiste algo?"

Did I *learn* something? That I can't trust him to keep his end of a deal, maybe. I keep my mouth shut while I sift furiously through my mental glossary of irritation, searching for words to tell him exactly how frustrated I am. Not coming up with any, I instead shoot Papi a glare that says, *Are you* kidding *me right now?* I hope that's clear enough.

His shoulders drop, and he shakes his head. "What can I tell you, m'ija? Those guys at the gas station must have forgotten their wallets or their appetites. Maybe both. I couldn't wait around for customers any longer. Let's see if they're hungry downtown." I don't know what to say to that, and before I can think of anything smart, I hear a *bam, bam, bam, bam* on my door.

"Huh?" I'm confused for a second, and then I realize who must be knocking. I crank down the window, and sure enough, it's Arthur Choi, all four feet ten inches of him—an even five feet with his hair included. He looks up at me and yanks his headphones down around his neck. They are bright orange and so big he looks almost like he's wearing a life preserver.

"Hey, Stef. Think I can get a ride to the library?" Usually, Arthur's mom picks him up from school, not because she doesn't trust him to walk alone, but because he lives so far away. When she has to work late, he goes to the library to wait for her, finishing his homework, reading his magazines, listening to his music. Without a chaperone. In peace. Arthur and I have known each other since kindergarten, back when his mom and my dad teamed up and trailed the school bus in her minivan anytime our class had a field trip. Unlike my parents, though, Arthur's seem to have noticed that he isn't five years old anymore.

I turn to Papi.

"Órale." He nods. It's a word that comes in many flavors. Sometimes it means "Yes," and other times "YES!"

Sometimes "Listen," and sometimes "I hear you."

This time it means "Of course!" and I slide to the middle of the bench seat as Arthur hops up next to me.

Finally, Papi starts the engine, and as soon as he does, his banda music comes bouncing out of the speakers and pouring—I'm sure of it—right through the open windows. Unfazed, Arthur bops his head right along to the *oompah-pah* rhythm. I slam mine back into the seat and squeeze my eyes shut.

"Please, can we just go now?"

CHAPTER
2

Papi pulls over at the curb across from the library. I expect him to leave the truck running while Arthur grabs his backpack off the floor of the cab, but instead, he parks, unbuckles his seat belt, and steps outside.

We can't be stopping here, I think, taking stock of the neighborhood on the other side of Tía Perla's windshield. No shoebox-shaped office buildings full of lawyers or accountants or real estate agents, their stomachs grumbling for a late-afternoon snack. No auto-repair shops with impatient walk-in customers looking for ways to kill time while they wait for their oil changes and smog checks. Nothing but neat houses with neat lawns, a basketball hoop in every other driveway.

Just behind the library, there's a small playground with a tire swing, a slide, and a couple of benches, and if you weren't an expert in taco truck terrain, you might consider it promising. But I know from experience that you could park for hours at a playground like that and be lucky to see even a dog walker or two. One of them might come up to the window, but just to ask for a free glass of water.

"Arturo," Papi calls.

Arthur lifts his nose out of his backpack, where he's been fishing for his library card. He squints at me, his scrunched-up eyebrows asking, *What's going on?*

"No idea," I say.

He opens his door, and we both climb down, following Papi's voice to the back of the truck. We find him at the cutting board, about to chop a bunch of green onions. Papi works quickly, dicing a tomato, sprinkling pepper. When he's finished, he presents Arthur with something that looks like a burrito, only it's wrapped in a giant lettuce leaf instead of a tortilla. "Prepared especially for you," he announces with a flourish. "The wheat-free, dairy-free, egg-free, nut-free, and meat-free super burrito."

Arthur is allergic to basically everything and is a vegetarian for environmental reasons. Sometimes, between customers, Papi experiments with new Arthur-friendly dishes, claiming the challenge keeps his kitchen skills as sharp as his knives. We add the best recipes to the Official Arthur Choi Menu, a note card taped to the door of the fridge. So far, there's a mango salad with charred corn and slivers of red onion; avocado halves stuffed with rice, green chili, cilantro, and bell peppers; and an almost-overripe banana, cut into coins and sautéed in margarine, brown sugar, and cinnamon until each crispy slice is floating in a rich, caramel-colored sauce.

I'm wondering what inspired this afternoon's lettuce-leaf burrito when I realize that if Papi had time to dream it up between customers, he really must have had a slow day with Tía Perla after all. *Aaaand* it's possible I overreacted about the whole gas station thing. I glance over at him. Papi looks up at me and winks before nudging Arthur to have a taste.

"Ándale," he says.

"Yeah, go on," I add, curious now. "Try it."

Arthur considers the burrito for a moment, then devours almost half of it in one enormous bite. Papi and I watch, hungry for his reaction.

"*Aww-oooohm*," he mumbles, cheeks puffed like they're hiding Ping-Pong balls. He swallows.

"Pretty good, Mr. Soto. Not as good as the bananas, but pretty good. Thanks."

"*Pretty* good?" Papi crosses his arms and cocks his head. "Pués, does it go on the menu?"

Arthur looks at me, looks at Papi, and grins.

"It goes on the menu."

"¡Órale!" Papi thunders, holding out his hands for Arthur and me to slap. "It goes on the menu. Specialty of the house."

As Arthur goes back to devouring his burrito, Papi locks Tía Perla's kitchen door and gives it a quick tap—the way you might congratulate an old friend with a pat on the back—then hops into the cab and settles into his seat.

Two bites later, when he's done eating, Arthur flashes me a peace sign and pulls on his earphones. Stick-straight tufts of spiky hair spring up around the orange band. "See ya," I say. Papi and I watch him cross the street. Not until the library doors part to let Arthur in, then close again safely behind him, does Papi start the truck.

"¿Vámonos?" he asks me.

"Let's go." I nod.

We drive to a convenience store downtown where the owner lets us use his parking lot as long as we send customers inside to buy their sodas. It's a fair deal. The little shop isn't the busiest stop on our route, but we know we can count on some regulars: commuters who pull in for tortas and tacos to tide them over on the drive home; gray-haired men in starched shirts who come to the store for lottery tickets and decide a burrito is a good bet, too.

While Papi lifts open the canopy, warms up the grill, and unfolds two steel chairs on either side of a salsa-stained card table, I drag my backpack to the spot at the cutting counter that he always leaves clear for me to finish my homework. He notices me sneaking a handful of corn chips, and before long, a quesadilla, cut into wedges and arranged around a dollop of chunky guacamole, appears on a plate next to my math book. People always ask if I get sick of taco truck food, if I'm bored eating the same thing night after night. But what they don't know is that it's never the same thing. Somehow Papi always prepares exactly what I'm craving. On the hottest days, when my bangs stick to my forehead, there are salads drizzled with lemon juice. When I leave school exhausted after a particularly tough history test, there's the comfort of a plain flour tortilla smeared with nothing but melting butter.

I spoon some guacamole onto my quesadilla and wonder what Mami's up to at home. Getting ready for work, I guess. She's a cashier at the open-all-night grocery store. You would never believe, she always says, what people need at one o'clock in the morning: a box of pancake mix, a birthday card, a cantaloupe. Most of the time, she doesn't get home until I'm already in bed, and since Mami and Papi won't even *think* about letting me stay home alone, I'm parked with Tía Perla until the dinner rush lets up—it feels like forever.

Finally, though, Papi taps me on the shoulder. He has scooped the last glob of sour cream onto the last super burrito of the day, and it's time to pack up Tía Perla. We take her to the commissary, where drivers from all over the city store their supplies and keep their food trucks overnight. I help him wipe down the countertops and rinse out the big plastic containers we use for storing onions and tomatoes. When we're finished, he tucks my backpack under his arm, and we walk together to our pickup. The lights in the parking lot blaze bright white against the inky sky. I'm wondering how I could re-create the effect with paint and paper when Papi jokes, "Say buenas noches to Tía Perla." I yawn and wave—she looks a little out of place parked next to so many other trucks with flashier paint jobs and shinier chrome bumpers, her tired headlights pleading with us not to leave her behind.

CHAPTER
3

I can remember the day Papi brought Tía Perla home and parked her in the driveway early on a Saturday morning. Mami had been pacing the living room. She wore her green silk dress and black heels as though she were on her way to a party, or to meet someone important. I sat on the couch in the itchy gray skirt I usually saved for church. When she heard Papi honk the horn, she squealed, tucked a stray curl back behind my ear, and grabbed both my wrists.

"They're here!" I yelped.

"¡Aquí están!" she echoed. The two of us ran outside together.

Mami cleared all three front-porch steps in one eager hop, then stopped short on the lawn and wrinkled her nose. After listening to Papi gush about the truck—the flattop grill and four-burner stove, the stainless-steel walls and brand-new tires—we were expecting a beauty, a champion purebred. This truck looked more like a scruffy shelter rescue, in need of a warm bath and a loving home. The tires *were* brand-new, but everything else seemed dented or dusty. Still, Papi stood smiling in front of the truck, his chest puffed up proudly, his hands planted on his hips. Mami and I looked at each other, then we smiled, too.

Until that Saturday morning, Papi had worked as a house-painter for a big construction company. He had to leave the house early, sometimes before the streetlights had flickered out, and he always came home with aching shoulders. At night, after he and Mami had sent me to bed, I would hear them whispering at the kitchen table: "But if I could start something of my own..."

After a while, those kitchen-table whispers grew into a roar of plans and daydreams. Standing over the stove, refrying beans, Papi would suddenly burst, "When I open my restaurant, I'll serve all kinds of beans—not just refritos, but black beans and frijoles de la olla, too." His mother, my abuelita, had taught him to cook when he was my age. She didn't know where he might travel someday, she told him, but wherever he went, he would have her recipes to bring him back home. Now, nothing made Papi happier than sharing that warm at-home feeling with others.

Mami would spoon Papi's homemade salsa onto her breakfast eggs, take a bite, and then, with her mouth still half-full, exclaim, "Mi amor! At your restaurant, you *must* make your own salsa. Promise me, nothing from a jar."

And one sunny afternoon, when I poked around the refrigerator looking for something cool to drink, I asked, "Papi, can there be strawberry soda at your restaurant?" He swept me off the floor and lifted me over his head.

"Órale!" he shouted. "Strawberry soda! Orange soda! Grape soda!"

I giggled, my braids dangling over Papi's nose. "Lime soda! Mango soda! Cherry soda!" Mami shook her head at us and poured me a glass of ice water.

That's when we started saving. When the daydreams became so real we could taste them, as sweet and fizzy as strawberry soda.

Scrimping was harder than I thought it would be, but also a little like a game with all of us pitching in to pinch pennies. Breakfast, lunch, and dinner we ate plain beans wrapped in corn tortillas—so many that I still can't stand them. Mami stitched patches over the rips in my jeans instead of buying new ones. She also took in sewing projects from the dry cleaner's around the corner, gathering needle and thread after dinner and settling down to repair a seam or fasten a button. I thought I could make some extra money, too, maybe walking dogs or pulling weeds. Mami and Papi said no to that. Instead, they put me in charge of making sure we never left the lights on in an empty room, and agreed to let me chip in the nickels and pennies I had stashed in my piggy bank. I poured a silvery stream of coins onto the coffee table, and as the three of us sorted them into cardboard rolls from the bank, Papi put his hand over mine and said, "Gracias."

We worked and saved, worked and saved—for a little more than a year—until one day, while she was reading the newspaper, Mami stopped and said, "Hmmm." She waved Papi and me over and pointed to a small ad in the corner of the page:

FOOD TRUCK FOR SALE. USED, GOOD CONDITION.

"Hmmm," Papi and I agreed. It wasn't a restaurant, but it would be ours and we had saved just enough. "It wouldn't hurt just to look," he said.

Two weeks later, the truck was in our driveway.

The previous owner had called it La Perla del Mar, the Pearl of the Sea. The name was painted in loopy blue letters across one side of the truck, and it was the only thing that Papi thought really needed fixing. La Perla del Mar sounded like seafood, he thought, and that wasn't the food that brought him back home. We sat on the lawn, Mami spreading Papi's jacket out between the grass and her green dress, and tried to come up with a new name.

"Señor Salsa," Mami proposed.

I groaned.

"Holy Frijoles," Papi suggested.

I threw a clump of dried grass at him. He ducked and laughed.

And then it came to me. "Tía Perla."

My parents looked at each other, not sure whether we were still joking. "No, really," I said, standing up and dusting off my skirt. "Listen." It was a name that sounded like home, I told them. Like food cooked from scratch by your favorite aunt. "Plus, we won't have to repaint the whole thing."

Mami tilted her head right to left, my idea rolling around her mind like a marble. "Tía Perla," she said.

Papi nodded, slowly at first and then feverishly. "Órale!" he growled, hugging Mami and me tight. "Órale!"

We congratulated ourselves for a few happy minutes until Papi slapped his palm to his forehead. "Almost forgot!" He climbed back inside the truck and returned with three bottles of strawberry soda. Tía Perla was home and officially part of the family.

Over the next few weekends, we painted over the sea-scape that had been airbrushed onto the truck's side, replacing it with bunches of red and white roses. We covered up most of the old lettering, too, everything but PERLA. Papi had lifted me onto a stepladder and handed me a paintbrush. In careful blue strokes, I wrote TÍA.

Five years later, our paint job is faded and chipped, and palm trees from the old seascape are peeking through in places. It needs touching up, I think, as I sketch in the margins of my social studies notes. But who's going to do it? I certainly don't want to spend any more time with Tía Perla than I absolutely have to.

CHAPTER
4

Julia's house, behind a tall wrought iron gate, looks like it belongs on a different planet than mine, which is small and painted pink. But really, it's only a few blocks away. Our grandparents were friends back in Mexico, and it was Julia's dad who owned the construction company where Papi used to work. When we were little, before Tía Perla, Mami used to drive Julia to school every morning and bring her back to our house every afternoon. Julia and I would haul Mami's old purses and dress shoes to the front porch and pretend we were actresses. Or bankers. Or spies. Julia always decided, but it was always pretty fun.

Then, when we got to seventh grade, Julia decided she was

too old for a babysitter and persuaded her parents to let her take the bus to school. Not the school bus—the *real*, public bus. She's the only one in our class who does, and it's just about her favorite thing to talk about. She flutters into class seconds after the bell rings, blows her bangs off her forehead, and sighs, "Oh, Ms. Barlow, I'm so *sorry* I didn't get here in time, but my *bus* was running late." Like it's her own personal bus. Or at lunchtime, when she stands at the end of a table, tapping her foot on the linoleum until we all take a break from our conversations and look up. "You'll never *believe*," she begins, after she's sure she has everyone's attention, "what happened on my *bus*." Like anyone is even interested.

But the thing is, a lot of people *are* interested. Even me. It's like she's living the seventh-grade version of the glamorous lives we used to act out on my front porch.

On Tuesday afternoon, I see Julia in the hallway, yanking books from her locker and shoving them in her backpack. "I can't *believe* he kept us after class," she fumes to Maddie, who's leaning against the lockers and coiling glossy black hair around her finger. Maddie is new this year and glued herself to Julia on the very first day. Arthur knows her from Sunday school, but still, she pretty much left her old reputation behind when she came to Saint Scholastica. Was she first pick or last when they chose teams in PE? Was she ever sent home with head lice? Did she always win the spelling bee? If she started wearing feathers in her hair, would everyone else start

19

wearing feathers, too? We don't know. Maddie has nothing to live down and nothing to live up to. I'm more than a little jealous.

"Urrgh," Julia grumbles when she can't get her backpack zipped. "I'm going to miss my bus."

I consider pretending I didn't hear, but she seems really upset, so I stop next to her locker. "Julia, if you need a ride, my dad can take you home."

Julia and Maddie lock eyes for a moment. "No, thanks." Julia blinks. She slings her navy-blue cardigan over her shoulder and goes back to wrestling with her backpack.

I shrug and walk down the hall. I'm only a few steps away when I hear Maddie ask, "Why don't you just go with her? Didn't you used to carpool or something?"

Julia slams her locker shut. "Seriously? There's just no *way*. I mean, Stef and her truck smell like old tacos. What is she, the Taco *Queen*?"

I don't turn around. I pretend not to hear, but my cheeks burn. Julia's always been bossy and kind of a show-off, but never straight-up mean. I glance right and then left. No one's looking, so I pull my ponytail over my shoulder, bury my nose into it, and take a cautious sniff. Vanilla citrus-blossom shampoo. So there.

But I have to admit, isn't there just the faintest whiff of burnt tortilla mixed in? As soon as Papi and I get home a few hours later, I change out of my uniform and throw all of it—white blouse, plaid skirt, blue cardigan—into the dryer with three lavender-breeze dryer sheets just to be safe.

I try not to let Julia get to me, but after a week, I'm still not convinced I don't smell like Tía Perla. Before school starts, I wait outside our classroom with my sweater balled up under my arm. I stop Arthur and Amanda before they can step inside. "Come over here," I demand, taking them by their wrists and dragging them around the corner.

"Now smell this." I shove the cardigan under their noses. They look at each other, then back at me. "Go on," I say, shaking the sweater. "Smell it."

They both take a sniff.

"OOO-kaaay?" Amanda looks up. "That was *awesome*, Stef, and totally not weird at all. Are we allowed to go to class now?"

"But does it smell like tacos?" I demand, shaking the sweater again. "Am I the Taco Queen?"

Arthur had just taken a gulp of orange juice from a cardboard carton. It shoots out of his nose and across the tile floor as he bursts out laughing. "Taco Queen?" he sputters, wiping his hand across his lips.

Amanda considers it, then leans in for another smell. "Not tacos," she confirms. "But I like it. What detergent do your parents use?"

I roll my eyes. No help at all. As we're walking to Ms. Barlow's room for language arts, I tell them what I overheard Julia say. Arthur can't stop laughing, but Amanda groans. "Why would you even listen to her? You know she just likes being the center of attention."

I nod. "Yeah. I know, right?" Still, Julia's words cling to me like a stale smell. Amanda has her soccer team, Arthur has his music, Julia has her independence, and it seems like all I have is Tía Perla. Somehow, I have to find a way to wipe off the stains she's leaving on my reputation.

CHAPTER
5

Ms. Barlow is finishing a bagel and sipping from a cup of coffee when we find our seats a few minutes before school starts. She wipes a splotch of cream cheese off her lip as she smiles to greet us. "We're going to start with a writing exercise, so go ahead and take out your journals while we wait for the bell to ring."

I dig mine out of my desk and find a spot on the cover that I haven't already filled with doodles. It's almost always easier to draw my thoughts than to find words for them. The last time we wrote in our journals, I sketched a sailboat bobbing along atop curling blue waves. Now I add a sea monster, surging from the sea to swallow it whole.

"*Niiice,*" Christopher drawls. "Do my backpack next?"

I glance up and find four or five other kids looking over my shoulder. "Yeah?" I'm not sure Christopher is serious. I've been trying to spend more time working on my art. Sometimes I think I might even be getting better, but I'm not sure anyone else notices.

Suddenly, Julia's squeal from the back of the classroom yanks everyone's eyes off my drawings and reels them back to her.

"No way!" She shakes her head at her cell phone's glowing screen. She's the only seventh grader who's allowed to take it out of her backpack in the classroom—her parents had insisted. They gave her the phone for safety reasons, like if she runs into trouble on the bus. She's supposed to text them when she gets to school and again when she gets home so they know she's all right. Not that she's told us all about it a million times or anything.

"What?" Christopher asks.

Julia doesn't answer. "No *way!*" she screeches again. "No way, no way, no way!"

She screams and hugs her cell phone over her heart.

Even Amanda is curious now. "Seriously. What is it?"

"This is going to be *so* amazing." She sighs, sinking breathlessly into her chair but still not giving any hints about what she's talking about.

I roll my eyes. If Julia doesn't want to say what's so amazing, fine. I'm not going to beg.

But that doesn't stop anyone else.

"Come on," Maddie pleads. "Tell us. What's going on?"

"Oh, no big deal," Julia finally teases with a toss of her auburn hair. "Just that Viviana Vega is coming to town and I'm getting front-row tickets to her concert."

Maddie screams.

"No way," I whisper to myself. I look over at Amanda, whose eyes are wide with envy or disbelief. Probably both. Only Arthur seems unimpressed. He shakes his head and opens up a music magazine. The only singers he cares about are singers no one else has ever heard of. And everyone has heard of Viviana Vega.

The bell finally rings, and Ms. Barlow settles the classroom down to call roll.

"All right, all right. That's enough, everyone. Julia, I'm not sure Viviana Vega qualifies as urgent—put the phone away, please. Find your seats. Let's get started."

When Ms. Barlow had passed out our journals on the first day of school, I had expected the usual "how I spent my summer vacation" kind of assignment. Wrong. The writing prompts she puts on the board are always surprising and sometimes strange.

WHY ME? she wrote once with no further explanation.

IF YOU HAD TO SPEND A WEEK LIVING INSIDE ANY
BOOK, WHICH WOULD YOU CHOOSE AND WHY?

WRITE A THANK-YOU NOTE TO AN UNCLE WHO SENT
YOU A CAN OF CHICKEN SOUP FOR YOUR BIRTHDAY.

Compared with that one, today's question seems almost
normal: IMAGINE YOU CAN TIME TRAVEL, BUT YOUR PARENTS
DON'T BELIEVE YOU. HOW WOULD YOU CONVINCE THEM?

I can't convince my parents of anything. I feel like I have
plenty to say about today's question, but every time I bring
my pen down to write something, the words vanish. Instead,
I sit scribbling robots and rocket ships in the margins of my
journal until Ms. Barlow comes down the aisle in her white
canvas sneakers, taps me on the shoulder, and whispers, "Just
start somewhere, Stef. *Any*where. Sometimes starting is the
hardest part. It's easier after that."

I nod and begin. "I can't convince my parents of anything."

CHAPTER
6

After language arts, I have math, and after that, a ten-minute break before science, where Mrs. Serros divides us into pairs for an experiment—with baby diapers.

"We're going to continue talking about polymers, which you'll remember are long strings of molecules that can have some very interesting properties," she explains, walking up and down the aisles and around the desks. "Some bounce. Some stretch. Some are tough and rigid. Today you'll work with a superabsorbent polymer. See if you can figure out why it's called 'superabsorbent.'"

We cut our diapers open, revealing a grainy white powder

that we collect in Ziploc bags. When we drop water onto the powder, the granules swell into big blobs.

"Talk to your partners," Mrs. Serros says. "Besides in a diaper, where else might a superabsorbent polymer be helpful? How might you use it in a garden, for example?"

My partner, Jake, pokes at the glob of diaper gel on our table. "Sick," he says. I don't know if he means "gross" or "cool." It's kind of both.

The subject of Viviana Vega doesn't come up for the rest of the morning, but by lunchtime, the whole school knows about her concert, and tickets are all anyone is talking about.

"So," Amanda says, smacking her lunch tray down on the table where Arthur and I are already sitting. "According to *Julia*, the 'cheap' seats"—she puts air quotes around "cheap"—"are forty dollars each. I have ten dollars left over from my birthday. Where are we going to get the rest?"

"You could try selling a kidney," Arthur mutters drily, taking his veggie burger patty out of its bun. "You have two."

Amanda sticks her tongue out at him, then turns back to me. "I'm serious, Stef. We have to be there. I don't want to hear all about it from *Julia Sandoval*. We're figuring this out. Like, today."

Just like that, she stands up again, jamming a granola bar in her pocket before I can say anything. If Amanda were a polymer, she'd definitely be the kind that bounces.

She's right, though—it's a lot of money. But paying for tickets isn't our only problem, maybe not even our biggest problem. There's no way Mami and Papi are going to let me go to that concert without them—and there's no way I'm letting them come along with me.

We go from lunch to PE, which seems cruel. All I want to do is nap. But at least it's just kickball today. After PE is social studies and finally, because it's Tuesday, art.

Most people, if you asked them what their favorite day of the week is, wouldn't say Tuesday. It's still early in the week, and Friday is a long way off. There's nothing special about Tuesday. Except, for me, there's art class. And in art class, I never hear Mami's voice telling me I'm too young, or Papi's nagging me to be careful. *I* am in charge of the blank piece of paper in front of me, and I can turn it into something as vivid and adventurous or as quiet and calm as I want. There aren't any restrictions. Except Mr. Salazar's, of course. But that's different.

Pinned to the walls of Mr. Salazar's studio are a decade's worth of sketches and paintings, some yellowing, their corners creased. Smears and spatters of paints and pastels stain the tabletops, and dried-up clay is ground into the tiled floor. But our paintbrushes are always clean, organized by shape and size in old soup cans. We sit on tall stools at broad tables instead of desks and chairs. We can talk as much as we want as long as we get our work done.

We hang our backpacks off a row of hooks just inside the door to keep them clean and out of the way. Then we pick out smocks from a bin near Mr. Salazar's desk. The smocks are actually old button-down shirts with ink stains on the pockets or holes in the elbows, donated by parents or by Mr. Salazar himself. I pick out one with pink and green pinstripes and put it on backside-front.

"Grab a brush and fill up a cup of water on your way to your seats," he tells us. Then he asks me to pass out watercolor trays. I come up short, and he frowns. "Maddie, will you share with Julia?" The girls nod. "And, Stef, do you mind sharing with Amanda for today?"

Once we've all settled on our stools, Mr. Salazar takes a basket full of white crayons and sends it around the classroom. We each take a crayon and pass the basket along as he tapes a piece of watercolor paper on the whiteboard and begins the day's lesson.

"Who can tell me what 'resist' means?" he asks, his back to us while his hand darts over the page. Whatever he's drawing is invisible from where I sit, white wax on white paper.

"To fight back!" Arthur calls out, pumping his fist in the air. Mr. Salazar nods, without looking away from his work.

"Anyone else?"

"To push away?" I venture.

Mr. Salazar turns around and points a finger, first at Arthur, then at me. "Right and right. Very good, both of you. Today we're going to be practicing a technique called wax *resist*." He swizzles his paintbrush in a plastic cup of water, then dabs it on a cake of paint. "And here's why."

He brushes a wash of violet over the paper, then switches to blue and then to green. The colors bloom on the page. They spill into one another in liquid bursts—except for where Mr. Salazar had sketched with his crayon. The mystery drawing turns out to be a spiderweb, its strands gleaming white through all that color.

Is the wax holding back the free-flowing paint, keeping it from going where it wants to go? No, I decide. It's something else. The wax is shining through, bold and bright and refusing to be painted over. Julia seems to have read my mind.

"It's wax *resist* because the wax is resisting the paint!"

"Exactly!" Mr. Salazar claps. He tells us to spend a few minutes planning before practicing the technique ourselves. But I already know what I want to paint: parking lights glowing against the dark purple sky over the commissary at night.

CHAPTER
7

As usual, Tía Perla is waiting for me when school is dismissed, but this time, Papi has her parked just across the street. Progress. I wave to show him how much I appreciate it. Instead of waving back, Papi points his finger up and down the street and then points at his eyes, which I take as some signal to look both ways. So much for progress. Amanda follows me out, talking so fast about Viviana Vega tickets that it's hard to keep up. I'm surprised when she starts crossing the street with me.

"Hold up." I clamp my hand on her shoulder so she'll stop and take a breath. "Don't you have practice?"

"We have to run an extra lap for every minute we're late." She checks her watch and shrugs. "Worth it."

Papi is standing next to the truck holding sodas when we get to the other side. Amanda shakes her head. "No, thanks. Practice." Then she launches right back into concert talk.

"Okay, so I know Mom and Dad aren't going to just *give* me money for Viviana Vega tickets, but maybe, like, an advance on my allowance? Orrrrr, I don't know, a yard sale? I could get rid of all those stupid stuffed animals. And your drawings! You could sell some, Stef. That's at least a few bucks."

"Yeah," I say weakly, wishing she wasn't doing this right in front of Papi. I need some time to prepare my case, even if it *is* hopeless.

I feel Papi staring at me. If I can't keep up with Amanda, he must be completely lost. "What's all this about?" he asks in Spanish. "Who is this Viviana Vega?"

Amanda answers for me. "Mr. *SO*-to, everyone knows Viviana Vega."

"Es una cantante," I say quietly.

"Not *just* a singer. Pretty much the best singer ever," Amanda continues. "And there's a concert coming up, and Stef and I *have* to be there."

Papi nods but doesn't say anything. He just gets back in the truck.

Over the next few days, Amanda tries everything she can think of to raise the ticket money. I go along with her thinking wishfully, Papi hasn't said no.

At lunchtime, she goes without milk every day for a week—she even talks Arthur into giving up his orange juice—but when we count the change, it adds up to less than four dollars. Amanda teaches me to make her handmade headbands, and we sell a couple to girls on her soccer team but have to stop when we run out of old T-shirts. Amanda offers to babysit her little brother for five dollars an hour, but since she already has to do that for free, her parents just laugh.

By the time tickets go on sale, we're not even close.

There's really no way we could just forget about the concert, but it would be a lot easier if Julia wasn't reminding us all the time, wondering—too loudly, considering we're in the library—what she should wear and whether she should give Viviana flowers or a teddy bear when she goes backstage. Because, *of course*, she gets to go backstage.

With the concert sold out, Amanda and I try to decide what to do with the money.

"You have enough to download her new album at least," Arthur whispers. "I mean, if you don't mind listening to pop trash."

"Hey, Amanda," I say slyly.

"Hey what?"

"I think he wants us to download the album for him."

Amanda considers for a moment. "No," she says very seriously. "Give Arthur some credit. *I* think…he already has it!"

"And knows all the songs by heart?"

"Yeah, and sings them in the shower!"

We're trying so hard to hold back our giggles that they come out as tears. Arthur blushes, groans, and puts on his earphones, but not before the librarian catches him and gives him a stern look. Sheepishly, he slides them into his backpack.

I sock him lightly on the shoulder. "Don't be such a music snob." He socks me back.

CHAPTER
8

It's been so long since I've slept in on a Saturday morning that I don't really need to set an alarm clock anymore. Most days, my eyes just open at five o'clock. I stretch, change out of my pajamas, twist my hair into a lazy bun, and find Mami and Papi already in the kitchen. She has the newspaper open. He's pouring coffee into a thermos. Lots of parents spend Saturdays at ballparks and festivals and flea markets. Papi does, too. Only, he's there to sell tacos and burritos, tortas and tostadas. Saturday is his busy day, and it takes all three of us to make sure he's prepared.

The farmers' market is our first stop, and we leave as soon

as I gulp down a bowl of cereal. Papi pulls a notebook from his shirt pocket and leafs through it to find this week's grocery list while Mami walks over to a food stand. She comes back with three steaming cups of hot chocolate and hands me one. The first sip burns my tongue, but it's worth it. "So, what do we need?" I ask, feeling warmer and finally awake.

We gather onions, garlic, lettuce, tomatoes, and beans. We have everything else we need back at the commissary. When we get there, I head straight for one of the enormous refrigerators in the prep kitchen, my reflection fuzzy and warped on its stainless-steel door. I find the drawer assigned to Papi, pull out a bunch of cilantro, take it to a counter, and start chopping. Meanwhile, Papi, wearing disposable gloves, ladles salsa into teensy plastic containers. We leave the onions to Mami. They never make her cry. No one else is in the cavernous kitchen yet. The only sounds I hear are the soft thuds of knives on cutting boards until, after a while, Mami starts to hum.

"Estefania," Papi says finally, clearing his throat. "If you don't have any other plans, I'd like for you to come and help me today."

I don't have any plans, but if I did, they wouldn't involve Tía Perla.

"Well, I mean, there's homework, and I..."

"Órale," he insists. "I can really use your help, m'ija. We'll start at the park. Maybe you'll see Amanda play."

I guess I don't have a choice. "Fine."

Finished in the kitchen, we pack up Tía Perla and drop Mami off at home. It's still morning when Papi and I get to the park, but already the sun is beginning to bake the grass fields. "Good thing we restocked the soda," I say.

"Órale," he answers. I take orders while he cooks on the flattop grill—first, eggs and sausage for breakfast burritos, and a few hours later, chicken and steak. He wipes sweat off his forehead with his sleeve and whistles along to the radio on the counter.

"Two super burritos, no beans, and one chicken taco, extra jalapeños," I call back to him. "Eleven fifty, please," I tell the lady standing at the order window. "Any lime or salsa?" She fans herself with a baseball cap while waiting for her order.

Between customers, I watch Amanda's game at the far end of the park. From here, the players are just blurs of orange and green, but I recognize Amanda's two brown braids flying out behind her. I figure she's spotted Tía Perla, too—who can miss her?—and that later she'll jog over for a postgame bottle of cherry soda. I bury one way down at the bottom of the ice chest so it'll be slushy-cold when she gets here.

Amanda started coming to Saint Scholastica in fifth grade, but since we weren't in the same class, I didn't really meet her until sixth grade, when my parents signed me up for soccer. Amanda and I ended up on the same team. I had

hardly even kicked a ball before, but Amanda had been playing soccer almost since she learned to walk. She was fast, and
her passes always landed exactly where she wanted.

Scrimmaging at practice one afternoon, Amanda broke
away at the half line with no one but me between her and
the goal box. As she dribbled past, I turned, flustered, to our
coach. "Catch her!" he yelled.

I took off, running as hard as I could, Coach yelling, "Go!
Go!" behind me. I closed some of the gap between us, but I
could tell I wasn't going to get out in front of Amanda—she
was just too fast. We ran a few strides side by side, and then,
just as she was about to speed off again, I kicked blindly, hoping to find the ball and send it out of bounds.

Instead, I found Amanda's cleat, knocking her legs out
from under her. She landed with a smack and a howl and had
to sit out the rest of the season. I figured she would stop showing up for games and practices after that, but she was there
for every one, glaring at me from the sideline, her broken
arm resting on her lap. I tried to avoid her. But one morning,
as I was shuffling off the field at halftime, she said, "Hey."
I looked over to where she was sitting, still suited up in our
team uniform, complete with shin guards, even though she
wasn't going to play. I was surprised and a little scared.

"You're kicking the ball with your toe," she said, picking at
the grass instead of looking at me.

"So?"

She looked up. "So, you're supposed to kick with your shoelaces."

"My shoelaces?"

Amanda stood, found a practice ball, and demonstrated. "When you kick with your shoelaces, it's easier to make the ball go where you want." She kicked, sending the ball straight to my feet.

"Wow. Thanks."

Amanda shrugged.

"It's cool you got a blue cast," I blurted. I had noticed it right away, of course, but had been too afraid to say anything until then. "Was it to match our uniforms? If you want, I can draw a soccer ball on it after the game."

She smiled. "Okay."

"And I'm sorry I knocked you over."

"I know."

I didn't play soccer anymore after that season—our Saturdays were just too busy with Tía Perla—but Amanda and I stayed friends.

Now, as the referee blows his whistle long and loud at the end of her game, I see the teams huddle and cheer, then line up to shake one another's hands.

"I'm going to take a break. Okay, Papi?"

"Stay close, m'ija," he says, still pushing bite-size chunks of chicken around the grill. I grab the radio and Amanda's soda and wait for her outside the truck. Her parents say she can hang out with us until her little brother's game is over and it's time for them to go home.

We sit cross-legged in the grass, Amanda sucking the juice out of an orange wedge as I twist the radio dial, listening for a break in the static. I finally find a clear station playing, naturally, Viviana Vega. I sigh, pick up a twig, and start tracing little pictures in the dirt while Amanda chatters about her assists and the fouls the referee should have called but didn't.

Then I hear something that makes me sit up straight and hold my hand out to shush her.

"What?"

I shake my head and point to the radio. "Listen."

"Oh, I know. Viviana Vega? I'm starting to think Arthur's right. I'm so over it. I just want her stupid concert to be done with already so we can talk about something else for a change."

"No, *listen*!" I snap.

Amanda stops talking as the DJ announces he's about to give away two tickets to the sold-out Viviana Vega show. "Be the fiftieth caller, and the tickets are yours."

"A phone!" Amanda barks.

I jump to my feet, scramble into Tía Perla's cab, and yank Papi's cell phone from the glove compartment. I should probably ask first, but there isn't time.

I dial the radio station, my fingers shaking, then press the speaker button. We listen: *Beep. Beep. Beep.*

"Busy." I sigh, hanging up.

"So try again!" Amanda orders.

This time it rings. And rings, and I don't believe what I finally hear on the other end.

"Congratulations, Caller Fifty."

No way.

"Hello? Caller?...Anyone there?"

I don't know what to say.

"Oh my god!" I mouth soundlessly as Amanda snatches back the phone to talk to the DJ. My mind is racing as I hear Amanda say, "Is this for real?...Thirteen....Oh, my mom can do it!...Thank you!"

She taps a button to end the call. "That's it," she says. "We're not eighteen, so my mom has to go pick up the tickets at the box office. Can you believe this? We're gonna see Viviana Vega!"

I pull her up from the ground by both arms. "We're gonna see Viviana Vega!"

We scream so loudly that Papi comes running out of Tía Perla, a spatula raised in his right hand.

"What's going on?" he asks, looking frantic and eyeing his cell phone where we tossed it on the ground. "Qué pasó? What happened? What's wrong? Estefania, is everything all right?"

I stop jumping and frown. Why does he always have to worry so much?

I let go of Amanda's hands. "*Nothing's* wrong." I huff. "We're just happy." I pause and take a breath. I'm going to have to be careful about how I explain this. "You know that concert? The one next weekend? Amanda just won a ticket! She gets to go!"

Papi squeezes his eyes shut and sighs. "Qué bueno, Amanda," he says, relaxing his shoulders.

"Yeah, but what's *really* great is we have *two* tickets!" Amanda bursts before I can stop her. "Stef can come, too, right? You *have* to let her."

I look at the ground and erase my little dirt drawings with the toe of my sneaker. I wish I'd had a chance to talk to my parents—to convince them that everything would be fine— before Amanda had said anything. But maybe, just this once, they'll understand what a big deal it is. Maybe they'll trust me enough to let me go. I look up at Papi.

He is already looking at me, confused and maybe a little sad. I seem to be getting that look a lot lately.

"I see," Papi says slowly. "We'll have to talk about that. For now, m'ija, it's time for us to go. Good game, Amanda. Come on back to the truck and take some tacos for your parents."

Papi walks back to Tía Perla, and Amanda whispers, "They're going to let you go, right? I mean, Stef, this is, like, once in a lifetime."

After Papi hands Amanda a brown paper bag stuffed with tacos and salsa and tortilla chips, he and I leave the park and drive to the flea market. His lips are pressed together in a tight, straight line. Once, at a stoplight, I look up at him. I want to tell him I'm smart enough, mature enough. But the words feel like paste in my mouth, and I swallow them all back down as the light turns green.

CHAPTER
9

We spend the rest of the afternoon at the flea market parked next to a truck called Gyro Hero. Our menus are so different, Papi had explained, that we're not really competing with each other, just giving customers more options. Late in the afternoon, he sends me over with two carnitas burritos. I come back to Tía Perla with two pitas stuffed with chicken souvlaki.

The line outside our window is never very long, but orders are steady enough to stay put. Not until we've sold out of carne asada do Papi and I leave the flea market and head back to the commissary. It is after dark, but still warm, when we finally pull in. I can't help daydreaming about the Viviana Vega concert: I've never won anything in my whole life—not even a goldfish at the school carnival. It was obviously meant to be.

And then I remember how hopeless it is, and my chest goes tight.

Papi shuts off the engine. "M'ija," he says, "you can wait here until I'm finished if you want."

A break from cleanup duties? I'm about to say yes, but I have a second thought.

"Nope," I say, straightening up and unbuckling my seat belt. "I can help."

I have only a week to show my parents I'm not a little kid anymore. I have to make them see how responsible I am, to convince them I'm not too young to go to that concert.

Papi looks surprised, but he nods. "Órale," he says, leading the way. I restock napkins and empty the trash. As I'm carrying a tub of sour cream from the truck back into the commissary refrigerator, I notice Papi and some of the other drivers huddled around a bulletin board, squinting at a letter that must have been tacked there sometime this afternoon.

"Regulations?" asks the owner of Tacos al Grullense. "Regulations mean they want to drive us out of business."

"Es nada," Vera Padilla insists. She swats at the letter as though shooing a fly. She and her sister, Myrna, drive Burritos Paradiso. Usually parked outside the gym, it's famous for

Myrna's caramel-topped flan. "They try this every few years. Nothing ever happens. Trust me; don't worry."

Papi sees me watching and waves me over. "Estefania, ven."

I join the others in front of the bulletin board, and he points to the letter. He doesn't have to say anything for me to know he wants me to translate. He speaks good-enough English, but when it comes to important conversations and official-looking paperwork, he doesn't trust himself. He always asks me. I translate at doctor visits and parent conferences, when letters come in from the bank or from the electric company. I'm used to it, but it still leaves me with a nervous pins-and-needles feeling in my stomach. When Papi says he needs my help with Tía Perla, I know he just wants some company. When he asks for help with English, it's like he really *needs* me.

I look up at the posting. MEETING NOTICE is printed across the top in bold capital letters. "It's from the city," I confirm. "And it's about new rules. It looks like . . ." I scan farther down and read "renewable every year" and "clean and free from damage." Doesn't sound like a very big deal to me. Tía Perla might not be the prettiest truck in the parking lot, but she's clean enough.

I step back from the bulletin board. "There's going to be a special meeting. All of you can go if you have something to say."

"Ah, don't bother," Vera grumbles. "Like I said, nothing ever happens."

Papi pulls out a notepad—the one he uses to jot down which ingredients and supplies are running low—and copies the date and time of the meeting.

"All done, Estefania," he says. "Vámonos?"

CHAPTER
10

Sunday is the only day of the week we spend all together, the only day Papi leaves Tía Perla parked at the commissary. And by Sunday, all of us need a break. Papi doesn't want to cook for anyone. Mami doesn't want to be on her feet. I just want to sleep in. So usually, on Sundays, after I finally wake up, we drive to Suzy's Café for the breakfast special.

But today, my alarm clock jostles me out of bed at five thirty. My parents are still asleep, and I go straight to work. I iron a week's worth of white school uniform blouses and hang them, smooth and starched, in my closet. I sweep the floors and start the coffee, and by the time my parents wander into the kitchen, I'm chopping peppers and grating cheese to make us omelets.

"Don't worry about the dishes," I tell Mami when I see her glance at the growing stack in the sink. "I'll get to them after breakfast. Now, sit down, sit down. Siéntense."

Mami looks at Papi, who just laughs and sits down. I pour two cups of coffee—adding a splash of milk to Papi's—and set them down on the table.

"M'ija, thank you, but what are you doing up so early? What's all this?" Mami asks, tightening her robe around her waist.

"Oh, it's nothing," I say breezily, tucking a flyaway curl behind my ear. My hair falls loose over my shoulders the way Mami likes it. "You have such beautiful hair, so thick and full," she always tells me, trying to get me to wear my hair down. "Thick and full" is just a polite way of saying "wild and frizzy," so I usually pull it all back into a ponytail. But Mami has *also* said I look older with my hair down, so today I give it a try.

"I was just thinking," I continue. "I'm old enough to cook and clean a little." I open the refrigerator and grab the carton of orange juice. "Now that I'm getting *older*, you can trust me with more responsibility."

Mami looks confused, but she smiles and sips her coffee. "Well, thank you for breakfast, Estefania," she says. "I'm impressed."

Papi clears his throat. "And this doesn't have anything to do with the concert on Saturday night?"

"Concert?" Mami asks, stopping midbite to look at me.

I take a deep breath, sit down in my chair at the kitchen table, and tell Mami about the Viviana Vega tickets: They just have to let me go. The arena is totally safe, and I can take Papi's cell phone just in case. Plus, Amanda will be with me—I won't even be alone, really.

Neither of them says a thing. I try, but I can't stop the whine that creeps into my voice. "*Please?* Everyone else in seventh grade gets to go out by themselves. They go to the mall by themselves. They see movies by themselves. They stay home *by themselves*. I swear, you can trust me. I'm very responsible."

"Estefania, we know how responsible you are," Mami says gently. "But I'm just not sure about this. I don't think I like the idea of you being out there on your own. At a concert? And at night? All those people?"

Papi obviously agrees with her. Were they even listening? I hold my breath for five long seconds to keep from rolling my eyes. This is almost the same conversation we had when I wanted to go on the end-of-the-year trip to the water park last summer ("Those slides look so dangerous"); when Amanda's parents invited me to go with them on their family camping trip ("What if there's an emergency and you can't reach us?"); and when the neighbor offered me twenty dollars to babysit her daughter for a couple of hours one weekend ("Taking care of little kids is a lot harder than you realize. Why don't you watch her here at home where we can help you?").

I let my breath out slowly. "Please. Just think about it," I say through gritted teeth as calmly as I can manage. My hand shakes as I pour myself some juice.

The rest of our breakfast is awkward and quiet. I take a few bites of my omelet and push the rest around my plate. It's not too bad, actually, but I'm just not hungry. After a while, Mami gets up to take a shower, whispering, "Thanks again, m'ija," and Papi opens the newspaper. It hardly seems like there's any reason to wash the dishes anymore—it's not going to make a difference with my parents—but even I think it would be pretty childish not to at this point, so I start filling the sink.

If it was a normal Sunday, I might be waking up right about now. We would come home after breakfast at Suzy's. Mami would call my grandma, handing me the phone to tell her about school. Papi would go out to his flower beds, and I'd usually go out and help him, or at least bring him a hat and a glass of ice water if the weather was warm. For dinner we'd eat leftovers, straight out of their Tupperware containers, and afterward, the three of us would fold laundry in the living room, catching up on the telenovelas we had recorded over the past week. Right now we're in the middle of *El Malcriado*. It's about a poor but beautiful housekeeper (of course) who falls in love with the rich but spoiled son of her employer (obviously). I'm betting that, in the end, a letter will come for the housekeeper, telling her she's inherited millions from a long-lost uncle. Mami thinks she'll end up saving the rich man's life, causing him to see how foolish he was to have ignored her all those years. "Then he'll beg her to marry him, right there in the hospital. Just watch," Mami predicts. Papi rolls his eyes at us, but we know he's just as eager as we are to find out what happens next.

But tonight, we don't get the chance. The uncomfortable hush that fell over us at breakfast lasts through the morning and into the afternoon. After her shower, Mami calls my grandmother, like she always does, and Papi goes outside to work in the garden. But instead of following him, I go to my room and close the door behind me. I finish the little homework I had left, then open my sketchbook. Drawing calms me, and I even start feeling hopeful. Mami and Papi haven't said no to the concert—maybe they're at least considering it. When I wander out of my room around dinnertime, I find Papi at the kitchen table with his grocery list and a reheated container of spaghetti. He looks up and holds it out, offering me a bite. I shake my head, and he goes back to planning for the week ahead. Not very hungry, I warm a tortilla on the stove, spread some butter over it, then roll it up to eat on the living room sofa. When Mami comes in with the laundry basket, I wipe my fingers to help her fold, but we don't turn on the TV.

CHAPTER
11

Amanda is waiting for me in the hallway outside our classroom when I get to school on Monday morning.

"Well?" she asks.

"Well, what?"

"Well, you know what. What did your parents say? Are you coming to see Viviana Vega? Stef, you *have* to come."

"Well, they haven't said no," I tell her, trying to sound optimistic. In my head I add, *"Yet."*

"Well, I talked to my mom, and she says you can come over to my house for dinner on Saturday," Amanda continues. "Then my sister will drop us off at the arena and *wait* for us right outside until it's over. I mean, she'll be *right* there, practically with us. That *has* to make your parents feel better, right? My mom can call your mom if you want."

"That's okay." I shrug. I wish that would help, but I don't think it will. Amanda's sister is seventeen. Almost an adult, but Mami and Papi won't see it that way.

As far as Amanda's concerned, it's a done deal. She's still talking about the concert and the songs she hopes Viviana Vega will perform as we walk into Ms. Barlow's classroom. It takes me a few seconds to notice, but everyone stops talking as Amanda and I hang our bags off the backs of our chairs.

"What?" we say in unison.

"Amanda, were you on the radio the other day?" Jake asks.

More questions fly at her, one after the other.

"Is it true you get to meet Viviana Vega?"

"Can you get me her autograph?"

"Who are you gonna take with you?"

Even Arthur, who still says he can't stand Viviana Vega, pulls his headphones down around his neck to listen.

Amanda winks. "Stef. I'm going with Stef," she says, pulling me toward her desk. "She's actually the one who called. It was her phone."

"Stef doesn't even *have* a phone." Julia sniffs without looking up from hers. But no one seems to notice. Before she can say anything else, class begins, and Ms. Barlow prints today's writing exercise on the board: "Describe what it feels like to be wrong."

After about fifteen minutes, she tells us that when we've come to a good stopping place, we can put away our journals for some free reading time. It doesn't happen very often, but ever since Ms. Barlow told me graphic novels count as books, I look forward to free reading almost as much as art class. I see Arthur slide his journal into his desk and pull a music magazine out of his backpack. The cover is ripped off, probably because his mom thought the picture was inappropriate for school. But she lets him read it anyway. Amanda grabs a book from Ms. Barlow's library, takes it back to her desk, turns a few pages, closes it, takes it back to the library, and chooses another. And then another, and another. I'm startled when the bell rings and I haven't even closed my journal. I've written three full pages, not on what it feels like to be wrong, but on finally convincing my parents I've been *right* about deserving some independence, and especially about deserving to go to the Viviana Vega concert.

We have a test in math, so there isn't time to talk about the concert. But in science, there's a substitute teacher, and while we fill in our worksheets, Amanda keeps whispering plans across the table. By lunchtime, I've caught her contagious optimism and can almost see myself at the arena with her. "I wonder if they'll let us take pictures inside," Amanda considers. Then she slumps—"I wonder if we'll be close enough to even see"—and recovers—"Oh well. I mean, at least we'll be there, right?"

"You can always try to sneak up closer," Arthur offers helpfully. Then he turns to me and tilts his head. "But, Stef, do you really think your mom and dad are going to let you go?" He knows better than Amanda what it's like to have overprotective parents.

"Of course they are—they have to," Amanda answers for me.

"They might," I say.

"Miracles can happen." Arthur shrugs.

And then, at the end of the day, an actual miracle actually happens.

I leave school and scan the parking lot, looking for Tía Perla. She isn't there. Not a trace of her.

No way.

Amanda jogs off to practice, and Arthur climbs in the front seat of his mom's sedan. I wave good-bye and start walking, a few steps behind Julia. She turns around when she hears me, and I flash a smile, even more sparkling-sweet than hers. She wrinkles her eyebrows and her nose—pretty much her whole face is scrunched up in confusion. Then she snaps her head back around, and her red-brown hair flutters down, smooth and straight over her shoulders as though nothing had ever disturbed it. She continues on to the bus stop without looking back. I smile again, for real this time.

I turn the corner and walk toward the gas station where I'm supposed to meet Papi. It takes me less than ten minutes to get there, and just like I've always said, absolutely nothing even remotely dangerous happens along the way. I'm considering whether to give Papi an I-told-you-so speech, or whether it would be smarter to act as though leaving school on my own was nothing out of the ordinary, when I notice Tía Perla parked alongside two other taco trucks. And that's definitely out of the ordinary.

These trucks aren't like Gyro Hero; they might look a little different than Tía Perla, but their menus are almost exactly the same. I could probably guess what they serve without even looking: tacos, burritos, super burritos, tortas, tostadas.... It's not good for anyone's business for taco trucks to be parked so close together.

When he sees me, Papi waves me over to where he and the two other drivers are standing under the shade of Tía Perla's canopy, studying a piece of paper.

"Does it really say we need bathrooms?" asks one of the men, shaking his head. "And we have to move every hour? This is going to put me out of business."

"Estefania, go inside and get a soda, then come out and read this for me," Papi says calmly.

I decide the soda can wait. The letter is addressed to Papi. It is stamped with the city seal.

"Dear Mr. Soto," I read out loud. "You are receiving this notice because you are an officially registered mobile food vendor. We are writing to inform you of proposed regulations that, if adopted, could affect your business. You are invited to attend a public hearing to discuss the attached proposals that we hope will maintain a quiet and clean environment throughout the city and will ensure the health and safety of all citizens."

On the next page is what looks like a list of rules for food trucks like Tía Perla. "Trucks must be parked within one hundred feet of a public restroom." Is that even possible?

"Operators must move their trucks every sixty minutes." That makes no sense. As soon as we set up everything, it would be time to pack it all in again.

"Permits must be renewed every year instead of every five years, and will be granted based, in part, on vehicle appearance."

I stop reading. This sounds just like that letter in the commissary. Maybe it really was serious after all.

"Papi?" I glance up, searching his face for clues about whether we should worry. He looks like he's still trying to decide, and even though I've just finished translating for him, I ask, "What does this mean?"

"It means we're all out of a job," one of the other drivers grumbles.

Papi takes the letter, folds it, and tucks it back inside the envelope. "It's going to be all right," he says finally. "We'll go to this meeting, and we'll explain it to them. No one is out of a job."

The other drivers leave, and Papi, Tía Perla, and I stay at the gas station for the rest of the evening. I decide not to bring up the Viviana Vega concert, and Papi doesn't, either.

CHAPTER
12

When I hear Mami filling the coffeepot with water on Tuesday morning, I kick myself out of a tangle of blankets and sheets to join her in the kitchen. I've been up for hours, tossing and turning and playing out long, impassioned arguments in my head. Finally, I had resolved to demand an answer to the Viviana Vega question this morning, before leaving for school. My parents have already taken two whole days to think about it. That should be long enough. And anyway, Amanda needs to know whether I'm going with her. I pad down the hallway in socks and flannel pajamas, feeling sure of myself, ready to make my case.

Then I hesitate outside the kitchen door. As of this very moment, there's still a chance I might see Viviana Vega four days from now. After that, who knows? I'm not so sure I want to find out, but I take a breath and step inside anyway.

"You're up early," Mami says, half inside the refrigerator.

"Couldn't sleep."

She closes the door and turns to me. "Something the matter? You're not coming down with anything, are you?"

She steps forward and reaches out to press her hand to my forehead.

I duck away and sit down at the table. "*Ma*mi. No. I don't have a fever. I'm *fine*. It's just…"

Looking worried, she sets her coffee cup down and sits next to me. "What is it?"

I groan. What else can it be? "It's the concert. What about the concert?"

Mami sighs, but I can't tell what it means.

"Well? Are you going to let me go? Amanda gets to go. Her sister is going to be there. She'll be right outside the *whole* time." Suddenly, an even better argument occurs to me. "Julia is going, too. You *know* Julia's parents. They wouldn't let her go if it wasn't safe.…And I could borrow Papi's cell phone to check in."

Mami taps the edge of a spoon against her coffee cup. "Your papi and I have been talking about it."

"And?" I interrupt.

She raises an eyebrow. "And it's a very difficult decision, Estefania. He wants to talk to you about it himself. This afternoon."

I start to protest.

"This afternoon," Mami says firmly. "Now, go get dressed."

It's impossible to concentrate at school, where I spend all day trying to guess what my parents have decided. All morning, I'm feeling positive, convinced that if they weren't going to let me go, Mami would have just told me instead of drawing it out like this. But by the afternoon, I'm remembering how long it took just to persuade them to let me walk to the gas station after school. Asking to go to a concert is asking for a whole lot more, I think. And I decide it's a lost cause.

Only art class takes my mind off the concert. As we walk into Mr. Salazar's studio, we hang our backpacks on the row of hooks, same as we always do. But when we start picking smocks out of the bin near Mr. Salazar's desk, he stops us.

"No need for smocks, class. Our lesson today is going to be a little bit different. Please grab a seat and listen up."

Arthur and I choose stools next to each other. "Wonder what's going on," he whispers.

Once we've all settled, Mr. Salazar steps to the center of the room and asks Arthur, who is sitting nearest the supply closet, to open it up. I hadn't noticed before, but now I see right away that everything is running low. We're down to not much more than a stack of construction paper, a few jugs of tempera, and a dozen boxes of pastels—most of them missing colors.

"Not too many acrylics left," Amanda says to herself. It's true. There are only a handful of tubes, squeezed almost dry.

"Not too much of anything left," Mr. Salazar agrees. "And that's what I want to talk to you about."

It's a good thing that the supply closet is looking so empty, he assures us. It means we've been creating. Unfortunately, as we can see, there is very little left to work with and no money to buy more.

"I've been trying to figure out a solution for weeks," he admits. "Finally, I thought, You know, your students are intelligent people. Why not ask them for ideas?"

None of us says anything. Was he really asking for our help?

"Not all at once," Mr. Salazar jokes. Then he says he's sorry if he shocked us. "I thought that you were all mature enough to talk about this sort of thing—and I still do. I know that, together, we'll come up with a plan. So let's brainstorm: What do you think? What are we going to do to get enough art supplies to see us through this year and next?"

Maddie speaks up first. Twirling her hair around her finger, she says, "Maybe we can ask the art store to give us some stuff?"

Mr. Salazar nods. "The store made a large donation at the beginning of the year—that's where your new charcoal pencils came from. But, yes, Maddie, that's a good thought. We can ask whether they can help us out with some more supplies." He writes ASK FOR DONATIONS on the whiteboard. "What else?"

Christopher suggests we ask our parents for money.

"That's certainly an option. All of you have very generous parents," Mr. Salazar says. "But I was hoping you all could really take *ownership* of the problem."

Amanda raises her hand. When her soccer team needed to raise money to travel to an out-of-town tournament, she explains, they sold candy bars door-to-door.

I remember that. Mami and Papi bought a whole box that we ended up giving out for Halloween.

Mr. Salazar adds SELL CANDY to the whiteboard. "Any more?"

Amanda nudges Arthur. He thinks for a second, then remembers that when his church choir needed to buy new robes, they wrote letters to shops and restaurants asking for contributions.

"Good," Mr. Salazar says, scribbling WRITE LETTERS on the board.

Jake suggests a car wash. That's how his swim club raised enough to pay for repairs at their pool.

I think about how hard Mami and Papi and I worked to buy Tía Perla. The saving, the extra jobs, my piggy bank. I'm not sure how any of that would help our art class, though. Maybe if we all brought in our spare change...

But before I can say anything, Julia jumps off her stool, looking like whatever she has to say is about to bubble over like a shaken-up bottle of soda. "Okay. Guys. Those ideas? They're great and everything, but I've got it. I know what we should do."

She pauses, eyes sparkling as they flit from face to face. When she's sure she has everyone's attention, she bursts, "A dance! In the gym! We can charge admission."

The art studio begins to whir.

"We can sell cupcakes!"

"We can make decorations!"

Even Arthur is out of his chair. "I'll do a playlist."

I have to admit, it's a pretty good idea. "I can draw some posters," I offer.

Mr. Salazar holds up his arms to quiet us down. "This wasn't quite what I had in mind."

We groan, and he holds his arms up again. "Hold on, hold on. Let me finish. It wasn't what *I* had in mind. But it's *your* class, your art supplies. I'll have to get approval from the principal, but it sure sounds like we have a winning idea."

Mr. Salazar dismisses us, promising to have an answer from the principal by the time we meet again next week. "You better be prepared if she says yes," he warns. "You're in for a lot of work."

CHAPTER
13

Outside in the parking lot, Tía Perla is missing again. That's two days in a row. Not to jinx anything, but this feels like a good sign.

When I get to the gas station, Papi is helping someone at the window, so I let myself into the cab to drop off my backpack. There, on the middle of the bench seat, is a small package wrapped in the comics section of the newspaper. Taped to the top is a tag with my name printed across it in block letters. Curious, I peel away the paper and find a cell phone. I turn it over, part of me thinking it might be a toy. But no. It's real. I can't believe it. I had wanted one for my last birthday but didn't think it was even worth asking.

It's not as nice as Julia's. But still, it's a phone. It seems to be mine, and it's not even my birthday. What could have prompted a gift like this? I'm trying to make sense of it when I remember that Julia's parents gave her a phone for safety reasons—so she can check in with them when she gets to school and when she makes it back home. My heart starts thudding. Is that why Mami and Papi got me a phone? So I can check in with them? From the concert?

I leap from the cab, run around to the back of the truck, pull open the kitchen door, and throw my arms around Papi's waist as he's sprinkling cheese on an order of tacos.

"Thank you, thank you, thank you," I squeal as he hands the dish through the window to the customer below. "I can't believe this is actually happening!"

Papi thanks the customer, with an apologetic smile, then turns around to face me.

"M'ija, I'm so glad you're happy," he says, grinning.

"Happy? This is the best day *ever*. I have to tell Amanda. And don't worry. Everything's going to be fine. You can trust me."

Papi's smile droops at the corners. "Trust you?"

"Amanda's sister will take us straight to the arena, and she'll pick us up right after. You'll hardly even notice I'm gone. And, of course, I'll have the phone! I'll check in! As many times as you want!" I scream. "I can't wait until Saturday!"

"Wait, m'ija, wait," Papi starts, but I'm too excited to listen.

"I wish I could tell Amanda right this second. Wait! I have a phone! I can!"

Papi puts his hands on my shoulders. "M'ija, please. Stop."

Oh no. My stomach goes hollow.

"It's like your mami said the other night." He's almost whispering. "We think you're just too young for this. Maybe in a few years ... but, for now, we wanted you to have something special. This phone is a privilege. You've earned it. You have to keep it turned off during the school day, of course. And we don't want you calling your friends late at night, but we trust you. Plus, this way, if there was ever an emergency—"

I had stopped listening, but that catches my attention. "It's not even for *me*! It's for *you*! So you can keep *hovering*!" My heart is still racing, but now its *thump, thump, thump* is low and furious.

My eyes sting. I push past Papi, jump down from the truck, and take off, dropping the cell phone on the pavement. Papi yells, "Estefania! Stef! Wait!" But I don't stop. After a few moments, I hear him start the engine to follow me.

It doesn't take him long to catch up. But when I hear Tía Perla's horn, I don't stop. I don't even turn around. I keep walking, Tía Perla crawling along behind me, until I realize with irritation that I can't make it all the way home from here. I have nowhere to go. I'm stuck with Tía Perla. I stop and slump down on the curb. There's no way I can get back in that truck, not yet.

Papi opens his door. He'll come sit down; his voice will be gentle; he'll try to make me feel better. Or maybe he'll tell me this has gone on long enough and drag me back into the truck.

He does neither. Instead, he walks around to the kitchen. I hear him opening doors and pulling drawers. Then there's a minute or two of quiet before he gets back in the cab and just sits there. I guess it's up to me to end the standoff. I swipe my hand across my teary face, get up, and open the door without a word and without looking at Papi. On my seat is a skinny, foil packet. I know without opening it what I'll find: a tortilla rolled up with butter inside. Just looking at it makes me want to cry again, so I shove it aside and slam the door shut.

The next time Amanda asks me about the concert, I just shake my head, and she understands. "You don't even want my mom to try calling them?" she asks.

"It won't help."

Arthur gives me a poster that had been stapled inside one of his magazines. It's a blown-up picture of Viviana Vega performing at a concert, hundreds of arms reaching for her as she strides across the stage.

That's the last time either of them brings up Viviana Vega for the rest of the week.

CHAPTER
14

On Saturday, the day of the concert, I hear Mami and Papi in the kitchen, getting ready for the farmers' market. I don't get up to join them. I don't plan to leave the house. I might not even leave the bedroom. Still, I'm a little surprised when neither of them comes to wake me and Papi drives off on his own.

It's after ten o'clock when I finally get out of bed. I stretch and yawn and bury my bare toes in the shaggy brown carpet. I reach for the glass of water on my dresser and notice the cell phone sitting on top of it. I haven't seen it since that afternoon at the gas station and figured it was lost or broken or both. Papi must have snuck it inside my room overnight. For a second, I'm embarrassed about my taco truck tantrum. Then I look up at Arthur's Viviana Vega poster taped to my wall and realize this is as close as I'm ever going to get to her.

My eyes start to water all over again. I take down the poster, open up my desk, and pull out a sheet of drawing paper and a box of colored pencils.

I do what I always do when I feel like drawing but don't know where to start: Spill the colored pencils over my desktop, close my eyes, and pick a color without looking.

Orange.

Orange like a carrot? Meh.

Orange like ... the sun? Maybe.

Orange like a blaze of angry flames? That's it. I start drawing.

Orange flames ... shooting out from a rocket? No. Not a rocket, but a flying ... taco truck. I roll my eyes. Not even in my imagination can I ditch old Tía Perla. But maybe, at least in my drawing, she'll fly out of my life for good.

Soon, cottony blue clouds swirl above Tía Perla on the page. And beneath her, bright green vines with curlicue tendrils stretch to catch hold of her tires but don't quite reach. Here and there, yellow birds and purple butterflies dart over and under the flaming truck.

After what seems like only a few minutes, I hear a cautious knock on my bedroom door. I look over at the clock. More than an hour has passed since I started drawing, and by now, my page is nearly filled and screaming bright.

"Yes?" I answer. Mami comes in and stands over my shoulder.

"M'ija, it's beautiful," she says. "It's Tía Perla, no?"

"I guess." If she's trying to make me feel better, it's going to take a lot more than that.

She sits on my bed and smooths the quilt with her palms. "Stef, I know you're angry."

"Whatever." I'm not going to make this easy for her.

"And what I'm about to say is going to make you even angrier."

What? Not possible. I spin around in my chair to look her in the eye.

"The assistant manager just called in sick, and they've asked me to fill in at the store. It's a good opportunity, Stef, but I'm afraid I'm going to have to drop you off with Papi and Tía Perla so I can go to work. You still have a few hours before we need to leave."

She has to be kidding. There's no way that, on top of missing the Viviana Vega concert, I'm going to spend my Saturday with Tía Perla. "Why can't I just stay here? I'm sick of you treating me like a baby, and I'm really sick of that stupid taco truck."

Mami raises an eyebrow but not her voice. She takes one of my pillows and hugs it in her lap. "I know you think we're overprotective, but can you imagine what it was like for us, for Papi and me, when we first got here? We were older than you, but not by much. We didn't speak the language. We knew almost no one. We had almost nothing. Can you imagine what it's like to settle down in a place where you feel so … lost? To send a child into a world that still seems so far from home?"

"But …" I start to interrupt her. The world might be a big and scary place to them, with their just-good-enough English. But that's not me.

Mami shushes me with a pat on the hand. She stands up, then finds my hairbrush on the dresser and holds it out to me. "As for that taco truck, she helps pay for those pencils in your desk, those books in your backpack, that uniform in your closet, that paint in your art box. Have some respect for poor Tía Perla, Estefania. She's an important part of this family, and she will be for a long time if we're lucky."

Lucky? Not the word I would use. But it's no use arguing. I get dressed and pull my hair into a ponytail.

CHAPTER
15

We catch up with Tía Perla at the flea market. She looks the same as ever, of course, but something about her seems different and a little unfamiliar. Her open canopy had always seemed to say, "Welcome!" Now it doesn't say anything. Mami leans over to kiss my forehead, then waves good-bye to Papi before she drives away. Here we go again, I guess. I climb inside the truck to start taking orders.

When the flea market winds down and the line outside Tía Perla finally dwindles, Papi packs up the folding chairs while I wipe down the countertops. "Where to next?" he asks. It doesn't seem possible, but they're the first words he's said to me all afternoon.

"The park?" I suggest.

But the fields are mostly empty when we get there. We watch the first few innings of a softball game, but when no one comes to place an order, we decide to move on. It's the same at the convenience store and even at the gas station.

"Now what?" I ask.

Papi frowns. He taps his fingertips against the steering wheel and turns right at the next signal. The commissary, I think. At least we'll be home early and I can get back to my drawing.

But then he makes another turn and we're heading downtown again. What can he be thinking? We already tried the convenience store—all those downtown offices are closed for the weekend. We would have been lucky to get even a few customers this afternoon. Now that it's early evening, there's no chance at all.

It takes me a few more blocks to realize where we're going, and I don't believe it. A boulder lands in my stomach as Papi parks Tía Perla on the narrow street between a four-story parking garage and the arena where, in just a few hours, Viviana Vega will sing for everyone but me.

"No, no, no, no, *no*."

"Estefania, I'm sorry, but we really need the business. Who knows what's going to happen with these new regulations? We have to sell as many tacos as we can for as long as we can. We're lucky we got here before anyone else did."

I'm beginning to think my parents and I must have

completely different definitions of "lucky." This isn't lucky. This? This is a total nightmare. I can only hope that no one going to the concert notices me, the Taco Queen, stuck with Tía Perla. But, really, how can you miss us?

We serve a steady dribble of customers as the sun slowly sinks—early birds hoping for a glimpse of Viviana Vega and maybe even an autograph, desperate fans on a quest for last-minute tickets, even if it means paying a fortune. A little after five o'clock, Papi says he's going to cook the two of us an early dinner so we won't need a break when the real crowd shows up a little later. I want to tell him I'm not hungry, but the truth is, I'm starving. Just thinking about one of Papi's super burritos makes my stomach growl.

I stay at my post in the window while Papi cooks. Looking out toward the arena, I can just make out what I imagine is Viviana Vega's tour bus. I wonder what she's doing this very second. Warming up for her show? Posing for pictures with Julia Sandoval and anyone else who's *actually* lucky enough to have parents who don't worry so much?

Just then, a customer clears her throat outside the order window. "Hello?"

It startles me.

"I'm sorry. I guess I was kind of out of it. Can I help you?"

"This is probably going to sound crazy," she says. "But is there any chance you have anything on the menu that's wheat-free, dairy-free, egg-free, nut-free, and meat-free?"

Behind me, Papi laughs. "Órale," he says. "Specialty of the house."

I squint through the order window, half expecting to see Arthur. But it's just some lady with the hood of her sweatshirt pulled low over her forehead. "Sure. We can do that," I tell her.

Papi drops handfuls of tomato, onion, and bell pepper onto the grill, then squeezes half a lemon over them, conjuring a little cloud of steam. While the veggies sizzle, he unfolds a giant lettuce leaf, bigger than my hand, on the countertop. He spreads layers of guacamole, then rice, then beans over it, and heaps the vegetables on top. After adding a drizzle of salsa, he rolls it up like a burrito and wraps it in crinkly yellow paper.

I drop it into a bag along with a napkin.

"Four dollars, please," I say.

The lady pulls a bill from her wallet and hands it to me. "Thanks a ton. Keep the change, okay?" She's gone before I can ask if she wants a lime wedge.

I open my palm expecting to see a five-dollar bill. It's a fifty. This has to be a mistake. I open up the window as wide as I can and lean out. "Wait!" I shout. "You left too much!"

But the woman just waves over her shoulder as she jogs back toward the arena. "Wow, she must have really needed a burrito," I mutter. I show the bill to Papi.

His forehead wrinkles until, finally, he gives up trying to figure it out. "Well, you heard what she said, m'ija. Keep the change. You've earned it."

He must be feeling really bad about dragging me out here. It's a lot of money, and I'm not sure what I'll do with it. Maybe a few more posters for my bedroom? I might as well start decorating, since I'm never going to get to leave, I think resentfully. Or maybe I'll give it to Mr. Salazar. I wonder how many tubes of paint you can buy with forty-six dollars. Not enough for a whole class, I guess. But some anyway.

Then I remember what Papi said about business and needing to sell as many tacos as we can. I know I complain about Tía Perla. A lot. But I guess I've never really thought about what we would do without her. I punch the cash button on the register, and when the drawer slides open, I leave the fifty-dollar bill inside. "You might as well take this, too," I whisper to her.

CHAPTER
16

Eventually, the streetlights blink on, and a line begins to snake around the arena.

The line around Tía Perla is almost as long. There's no way Papi could have managed it without me.

"Four chicken tacos!"

"Two quesadillas!"

"One steak burrito, hold the beans!"

I'm calling back orders and counting out change with hardly a break between customers. The dinner rush is such a whirl that I almost miss Amanda and Arthur jumping up and down, waving their arms from the middle of the line. I'm surprised at how glad I am to see them—and surprised to see Arthur at all.

I poke my head out the window and mouth, *Come over!* We talk between orders.

"I thought you couldn't stand Viviana Vega," I tease Arthur. " 'Pop trash,' wasn't it?"

He sinks his hands in his pockets and looks away. "Well, Ms. Barlow said if I wrote a music review for extra credit she wouldn't give me a detention for wearing my headphones in class again. Plus, free ticket."

Amanda pokes him in the shoulder. "Whatever. We all know you're Viviana's biggest fan."

"And you're on a first-name basis?" Arthur pokes back.

Just then, a black limousine pulls up in front of the arena. Amanda points. "Think it's her?" she asks breathlessly.

"No way," I answer. "She wouldn't just walk in through the front door." Would she?

We watch as the driver gets out, walks around to the back of the limo, and opens the passenger door. Out steps Julia Sandoval, wearing a shimmering gold tank top and enormous sunglasses perched on her head.

"In case she has to hide from the paparazzi?" Amanda jokes.

"Obviously."

We watch to see whom she's with—which lucky seventh grader gets to spend the evening with Julia Sandoval and her backstage passes? I'm guessing Maddie, but the next person out of the limo is Julia's little brother. And then her mom.

Julia looks in Tía Perla's direction, but I can't tell if she sees us. She pulls her sunglasses over her eyes and walks toward the entrance with her family.

Papi comes over to the window with dinner bags for Amanda and Arthur. "You two be careful in there," he tells them. "Call us if you need anything. Estefania, you make sure they have your phone number."

"*Papi*," I whine.

"Oh, it's fine," Amanda says. "My sister's gonna wait for us, and Arthur has his mom's cell phone in case we need it."

See? I want to say. Instead, I bite my tongue and wave good-bye to my friends. Amanda promises to buy me a program, and they hurry off to join the line. I turn around again and notice that Papi has been watching me. He looks like he has something to say, but before he does, a face pops into the window.

"How fast can you get me a couple of tacos? I don't want to be late for the show."

Papi wipes his hands on the apron tied around his waist and heads back to the grill. "Two tacos," I say. "Coming right up."

CHAPTER
17

I open my eyes the next morning, still so tired you would have thought I had actually gone to the concert. Sunlight pours through the gaps in my mini-blinds, casting shadow stripes on my quilt. It's late, I can tell. Stretching under the covers, I'm surprised my parents haven't shaken me out of bed for Sunday breakfast at Suzy's. Finally, I yawn, twist my hair into a knot, and stumble into the kitchen, where I expect to find Mami and Papi drinking their coffee.

Instead, the kitchen is bright and empty. Two coffee mugs are drying on a dish towel beside the sink, and the only sounds I hear are the ticking of the clock and the hum of our neighbor's lawn mower. Weird. Maybe Mami and Papi are already working in the garden? Then I spot a note taped to the refrigerator door: DIDN'T WANT TO WAKE YOU, it says in Mami's neat cursive. GONE TO SUZY'S. CALL IF YOU NEED ANYTHING. I can't believe it and even peek through the blinds to see if my parents are actually hiding in the backyard or something. But it's true. I'm home alone.

No way.

Then again, considering that Suzy's is just down the block, they might as well be in the backyard. And it's only breakfast, after all. They won't be gone for more than an hour or so. But still, my parents have really left me home alone. I feel like I can do anything. And then I can't think of anything to do.

I warm a mug of hot chocolate in the microwave and take it to the living room with the newspaper. My parents have locked the doors and even closed all the curtains. It's dark and quiet, and really kind of strange without them. After skimming through the comics and gulping down my hot chocolate, I reach for the cordless phone, resting on the coffee table, and pull it from its cradle. Mami left a note there, too: IN CASE ANYONE CALLS, DO NOT TELL THEM YOU'RE HOME ALONE.

"I *know*, Mami," I say to no one but the ticking clock. Rolling my eyes, I dial Amanda's house. Now that it's finally over, I really want to hear about the concert.

Amanda's mom answers.

"Oh, hi, sweetheart," she says. "Amanda told me she saw you last night. I was so sorry you two couldn't go together.

But she and Arthur had a good time. They got home pretty late, though, and she's still in bed. Is it urgent, or can I have her call you later?"

I tell Mrs. Garcia that it's not urgent—I'll just see Amanda at school tomorrow. She hangs up, and I wonder what to do next. It's no use calling Arthur—he has Korean school every Sunday after church and won't be home for hours.

I rinse out my mug and go back to my room, guessing I'll just take a shower and then get a head start on my reading for the week. The front door opens as I'm brushing my teeth.

"Estefania?" Mami calls before the door has even closed behind her and Papi.

"In the bathroom!" I shout back, my mouth full of minty foam. "Just a sec!"

I find them waiting for me in the kitchen.

"Everything okay?" Mami asks.

"Of course," I answer breezily, like it's no big deal that they left me home alone for the first time in my entire life. "What could go wrong?"

Papi and Mami look at each other. This time, both of them roll their eyes at *me*. Then Papi holds up a take-out box from Suzy's. "We missed you at breakfast. You haven't eaten, have you?"

I haven't. And to tell the truth, I was starting to regret missing out on Suzy's amazing chorizo and eggs.

"Your favorite," Papi says, setting the box on the kitchen

table. Mami brings me a plate and a napkin while Papi goes to their bedroom to work on shopping lists for the week ahead. Mami sits down next to me as I shovel chorizo into my mouth.

"How did you get him to agree to that?"

"Agree?" Mami answers. "It was his idea. I was worried sick. I wanted to call you from the restaurant."

"Maaaaami, *seriously*," I whine. "You were, like, a block away. I was *fine*."

"I know." She sighs, squeezing my shoulders. "Now finish your breakfast, and then how about you press your school blouses like you did last week? And Papi's pantalones, too, now that we know you can use an iron."

If it means my parents are going to start treating me like a thirteen-year-old, I'll iron every shirt in the house, not to mention the pants. Socks and underwear, too.

CHAPTER
18

Mami is called in to cover another assistant manager shift on Monday morning, so Papi offers to drop me off at school. Since it's not our usual routine, and because we have to pick up Tía Perla on the way, I barely make it to school on time. Even though it's late, I had hoped to find Amanda and Arthur outside class, ready to spill all the concert details. But when I get to the door, I hear their voices already inside. I guess they couldn't wait to tell everyone else about Viviana Vega. I'm a little jealous I didn't get to hear first, but I guess I understand.

Stepping into the classroom, I see a swarm around Arthur's desk. Right next to him at the center of it is Amanda, her hands fluttering in front of her face. I try to piece together what she's saying and what she's so excited about.

"...I mean, we were there *right* after. We must have just missed her. I'm *so* mad."

Arthur sees me. "There she is!" Everyone turns around and stares. Everyone but Julia, whose eyes are fixed on the cell phone in her lap.

"What?" I look down at my shirt to see if maybe I spilled something in the rush out the door this morning. Looks clean. I pat the top of my head. Nothing sticking up. "Seriously. What?" I look to Arthur and then Amanda.

"What was it like?" Maddie demands all of a sudden. "Did you touch her?"

"Touch who?"

"Was she nice? Did you get an autograph?" Matthew asks. "Please tell me you got an autograph."

I look from face to eager face and can't figure out what any of them are talking about. Are they teasing me? Because my parents didn't let me go to the concert? But that can't be it. Arthur and Amanda are my friends.

I turn to Amanda again, my eyes begging her for a clue.

She stares back at me and blinks slowly. "You seriously don't know? Arthur, show her."

Arthur snatches a piece of newspaper from Maya, then holds it up for me to see. There, in black ink, is a picture of a taco truck that looks suspiciously like Tía Perla.

What now? I take the newspaper from Arthur, and everyone watches me read.

It *is* Tía Perla—and someone's outstretched arm passing a bag to a customer whose face you can barely make out under a dark hooded sweatshirt.

"I don't get it—wait."

I take a closer look at the picture and finally notice *my* outstretched arm. I remember the customer: wheat-free, dairy-free, egg-free, nut-free, and meat-free. I served her the night of the concert. It still doesn't make sense, though. Who would have taken this picture? *Why* would anyone have taken this picture? And how would it have ended up in the newspaper?

"But what . . . even . . . is this?"

Amanda, impatient now, takes my wrist and shakes it. "Come *on*, Stef. Look! Read!"

Okay, okay.

I look at the caption: POP STAR VIVIANA VEGA TAKES A BREAK FROM REHEARSALS TO SAMPLE THE LOCAL FARE BEFORE HER SOLD-OUT ARENA CONCERT SATURDAY NIGHT.

No. Way. I turn the newspaper clipping over, suddenly suspicious. "Is this even real?" Mami and I read the paper every day. We wouldn't have missed this. And then I remember, we didn't have time to look at the newspaper this morning.

Amanda starts laughing. "You didn't get to go to the concert, but you were the only one who got your picture taken with her. Crazy, right?"

Julia finally looks up from her phone. "It's a miracle she didn't have to cancel the concert because of food poisoning." But I don't even care. I can't take my eyes off that picture.

"So did you get her autograph, or what?"

"Did she say anything?"

"What did she eat?"

"Is she as tall as she looks?"

"Was anybody with her?"

I can't keep up. "No, I...I just, I didn't..."

"Oh my god." Julia smirks, her eyes flashing as she suddenly realizes something. "You didn't even know it was her. Viviana Vega came to eat at your crazy old taco truck, and you didn't even know it was her."

"Whatever. Of course I knew," I lie lamely. "I'm just, you know, surprised someone took a picture. Viviana wanted it to be a private dinner." Did I really just say that?

Finally, the bell rings, and Ms. Barlow gets up from her desk. "All right, that's enough. Everyone settle down and take your seats. If we have any extra time at the end of the period, Stef can tell us *all* about her celebrity sighting. For now, please open your textbooks to page one hundred fifty-nine."

As I pull my language-arts book out of my backpack, I turn around and whisper to Arthur, "Can I keep the newspaper to show my dad?" He nods yes.

By lunchtime, I'm not the girl whose dad drives a taco truck. I'm the girl who has met Viviana Vega. If you believe all the rumors, I'm the girl who has eaten dinner with Viviana Vega, who is practically best friends with her. It feels a little weird at first, but I get used to it. Quickly.

Our table is so crowded I have barely enough elbow room to open my milk carton.

"I mean, she's really down-to-earth for being such a major celebrity." (After all, she *did* eat off a taco truck, right?) "Viviana is just, you know, pretty normal."

I look across the table at Amanda and Arthur, double-checking that they're not about to gag. They still seem excited for me. Then for the first time all day, I notice the Viviana Vega button pinned to Arthur's polo shirt.

"I thought you couldn't stand her."

"Never underestimate the power of live music."

"Anyway," I say, looking around the table and nodding at Arthur. "He actually introduced us."

Arthur looks confused. I remind him of Papi's Official Arthur Choi Menu. "Specialty of the house?"

"Oh, yeah." He grins.

"If it wasn't for you, we might not have had anything to feed her."

Arthur straightens up on the lunch bench. "That's right," he says. "Viviana Vega's favorite dish is the Arthur Choi special."

CHAPTER 19

After school, I find Tía Perla at the far end of the parking lot, her front end peeking shyly out from under the shadow of a big ash tree. But since I'm still feeling so full of bubbles and butterflies to have (sort of) met Viviana Vega, it doesn't even bother me to see her there. When Papi honks the horn and waves, I wave right back, holding up the newspaper clipping.

"You have to see this!" I say, climbing into the truck. Papi takes the paper and studies the picture. Surprise crosses his face, and then confusion, as he recognizes Tía Perla but can't quite figure out why he's seeing her in the newspaper. I know the feeling and help him out.

"It was her!" I say, nearly jumping out of my seat belt. "Viviana Vega. At *our* truck! Crazy, right?"

"Ah, sí." Papi smiles. "Specialty of the house." He hands the paper back to me and starts the engine. "So you got to see her after all."

I shoot him a look that says *too soon*, but it dissolves quickly back into a smile. I tell him we should make a poster-size copy of the article and hang it up near the menu. This *has* to be good for business. Papi nods and says, "Mmm," but I can tell he isn't really paying attention. I'm a little frustrated that he doesn't seem to understand what a big deal this is when I realize we aren't heading for any of our usual dinnertime stops. I'd been talking so much and so fast I hadn't noticed.

"Wait, where are we going?" I ask. "Did you forget something at the commissary?"

"We're not taking Tía Perla out tonight," Papi tells me. "There's more important work to do."

If we're giving up a whole night's business, I think, this must be pretty important.

A few minutes later, we pull into the commissary and the lot is fuller than I have ever seen it. There are more kinds of food trucks than I could have ever imagined seeing in one place: Wok 'n' Roll, Lotsa Pasta, Dim Sum and Then Some, Heart and Soul Food. But mostly there are taco trucks, many

94

of them with vivid murals on their sides that make Tía Perla look even older and plainer than usual.

El Toro is a bright red truck with a giant black bull painted right in the middle, its head raised nobly as it gazes off into the distance.

A garland of red, orange, and pink hibiscus flowers creeps all the way around Burritos La Jamaica.

On the back of Mariscos el Nayarit is a swordfish leaping out of turquoise water, its knife-edged tusk pointing at a glowing sun.

The trucks are just like canvases, I realize, suddenly seeing them in a new way.

As Papi eases Tía Perla into a parking space, I unzip my backpack and start pulling out my math book, figuring I'll start my homework while he takes care of whatever important business he has inside. Instead, he tells me I better come along. He's not sure how long this will take.

I follow Papi to the warehouse where we store dry goods like beans and flour, and supplies like forks and napkins. Dozens of drivers are in there already, only none seem to be doing any work. They're sitting on upturned buckets and standing in groups of three or four. All of them look very serious, with hands shoved into pockets or balled into fists.

Papi stands near the back, folds his arms against his chest, and leans on a shelf. I find a bucket and drag it over to sit down next to him. Finally, Vera, from Burritos Paradiso, walks to the front of the room.

"Can everyone hear me?" she asks. I can tell she's nearly shouting, but from back here, her voice sounds small and flimsy. Someone calls out, "Louder!"

"I'll try to speak up." She nods. "Can you hear me? Can we come to order?"

Someone clangs a spoon against a big glass jar of pickles. *Ping, ping, ping.* The low rumble of voices peters out. "Thank you," Vera tells the man with the spoon. Then she turns again to face the group. "As you know, we're gathered here tonight to come up with a plan to fight these new regulations. I admit, Myrna and I didn't believe anything would ever come of it, but here we are. We have to take a stand."

There are murmurs of agreement, and the rumble threatens to build into a roar again. Vera holds up an arm like she's directing traffic. The rumble dies down, but my ears perk up. Regulations? Again? Papi had told the drivers everything would be all right. I believed him, and I haven't really worried much about it until now. I look up at Papi as he listens. He hardly blinks.

I pull on his sleeve. "You want me to translate?" I whisper.

He shakes his head and pats mine. "No, m'ija."

The city council, Vera explains, has scheduled a public hearing to discuss rules that will govern all mobile food vendors. "That's us," she says. "We need to come prepared to make a strong case for ourselves."

She reads the list of proposals I remember from Papi's letter. One by one, the drivers discuss them, deciding whether it's a rule they can live with or one they should protest. They trade arguments. They share stories. They decide they'll go to the hearing as a group. They'll bring their families and friends. They'll make an impression.

"Now, I know a lot of you are shy—you think your English isn't good enough," Vera says as the meeting wraps up. "But remember, if you want to be heard, you have to speak up."

We leave the warehouse, double-check that Tía Perla is locked up for the night, and walk back to our pickup. I wonder if Papi is going to speak at the big meeting—I can't really imagine it. I want to ask him if he thinks we really might go out of business. But he's gnawing on his fingernails, which gives me an even worse pins-and-needles feeling than when he asks me to translate. So I don't say anything.

When we get home, Papi asks what I'd like for dinner, but I tell him I'm too tired to eat and say good night. I kick off my shoes, flop on my bed, and stare at the ceiling, thinking a little about the meeting at the commissary. The situation seems much more serious than it did at first, and Papi's stiff arms, tight lips, and ragged fingernails aren't doing anything to convince me that everything's all right.

Then again, it's hard to worry too much about food trucks when I remember the newspaper clipping in my backpack. I get up to tape it to the wall, and for just a second, I let myself wonder whether it would be so bad to lose Tía Perla. Mami still has a good job, and maybe a promotion coming. Plus, Papi has switched careers before, hasn't he?

CHAPTER
20

In the art studio the next afternoon, Mr. Salazar doesn't leave us in suspense for long.

"I spoke to the principal about your fund-raising dance," he begins. We're perched at the edges of our stools. "*And ...* she says it's all right."

"*Yes!*" Jake slaps his hands against the art table, then winces. "Ow." Amanda is sitting between Arthur and me and happily socks us both in the shoulders. Julia and Maddie had been squeezing each other's hands, waiting for Mr. Salazar's verdict. Now they are off their stools, still holding hands and hopping on the linoleum. "*Eeeeeee!*"

"*If,*" Mr. Salazar continues, raising his voice over ours. "If you're really ready to take this on. Organizing a dance is a lot of work. And raising money on top of that? It's a tall order, is all I'm saying."

He suggests we elect a planning committee to help make sure we have all the little details covered. "Since this was Miss Sandoval's idea, she can be captain. Do we have a cocaptain?"

Mr. Salazar looks around as arms pop up around the room. "You're all leaders. But remember, this should be someone who has some spare time." Amanda puts her arm down. "Someone with creative ideas. Someone who knows how to throw a good party." Julia smiles at Maddie. "But, more important, someone who knows how to tell people why they should care."

Christopher shoots his hand up, but before Mr. Salazar even gets to him, he calls out, "Stef. Pick Stef Soto. Maybe she can get Viviana Vega to come."

"Yeah, right," Amanda, Arthur, and I say in unison. But voice after voice agrees with Christopher. "Yeah, pick Stef."

"What?" I ask, baffled and slightly terrified.

"What?" Julia sneers.

I can't believe it. And judging by the look on her face, neither can Julia.

Mr. Salazar hooks his thumbs in his belt loops and seems to think about this. "Well, Estefania? What do you say?"

I don't know. Working with Julia? Being in charge? And

what if Mami and Papi won't let me go to the dance? How would I explain *that*?

Then again, art *is* my favorite class. And this is a really great chance to be known for something besides Tía Perla. I look at Arthur and Amanda, who are both nodding enthusiastically. Amanda elbows me in the ribs. "Ow!"

"O*kay*," I tell Amanda, rubbing my side. I look back at Mr. Salazar. "Okay," I say. "I'll do it."

"Fine." Julia huffs. "You can be my vice captain."

"Cocaptain," I correct her.

Before Mr. Salazar dismisses us, he passes out permission slips, asking our parents to let us stay an hour after school twice a week to plan the dance. I fold mine in half and tuck it into my backpack. Before I show it to my parents, I better figure out how I'm going to persuade them to sign.

I grit my teeth all the way to the gas station and present the permission slip to Papi as soon as I get there. His lips move softly as he reads the letter, and I start to panic. They can't say no again. Before he can say *anything*, I start explaining about the empty art closet and how much I love art. I tell him that Mr. Salazar is counting on us—counting on me—to plan the dance and make it a success.

Papi puts a hand on my shoulder. "M'ija, calma." He chuckles. "Of course Señor Salazar is counting on you. I don't know if I like the idea of you going to a dance ..."

I feel my cheeks flush. But Papi checks himself and pulls

a pen from his front pocket. "You'll be at the school?" he confirms.

"In the studio for planning meetings. The dance will be in the gym."

"And there will be chaperones?"

"Some of the teachers." We're supposed to recruit parent volunteers, too, but I don't mention it.

Papi finally signs. I take the permission slip back from him and zip it up in my backpack before he can change his mind.

CHAPTER
21

Two days later, we herd into the art studio after school for our first dance-planning session. Amanda can't miss soccer practice, but she sends me to the meeting with a brown paper grocery bag filled with some of her mom's old craft magazines. "There are some really good ideas for decorations in there," she tells me, promising to work on streamers and garlands at home. "We can make them ourselves. I put sticky notes on the pages."

Once we're settled in the studio, Mr. Salazar reminds us that to raise the money we need, we're going to have to plan carefully and work quickly. He puts Julia, as captain of the committee, in charge of dividing the rest of us into teams, each responsible for some part of the preparations. It turns out to be the perfect job for her. Her first assignment is for me, her cocaptain, and it sounds like I'm in charge of taking notes and basically following her orders. She ignores me when I start to complain.

"Next, someone needs to be in charge of decorations," she continues.

I plop Amanda's bag of magazines down on the table. "Amanda's in charge of decorations," I say. "She already has some ideas."

Julia challenges me. "Amanda's not even here."

"She can work from home," I insist.

Julia tosses her hair impatiently. "Fine. Whatever. Amanda is in charge of decorations. Write that down."

We bicker our way down a long list of jobs until every post is filled but one.

"Publicity. The most important," Julia says, chin raised. "Obviously, if no one shows up, it doesn't matter how good the refreshments are, or what the decorations look like."

"And if no one shows up, we don't raise any money for art supplies," I add.

"I *know*. I was just about to say that." She pauses, waiting for everyone's attention. "That's why I'm in charge of publicity." She turns to me and smiles, sparkling-sweet. "You can still make some posters if you want." Then she murmurs, too quietly for Mr. Salazar to hear, "Just don't spill any taco sauce on them."

Maddie puts her hand over her mouth to quiet her giggles. My face burns, and I want to scream. Here I am, finally escaping Tía Perla's salsa-soaked reputation, and Julia has to keep reminding people of it.

Arthur comes to my rescue—or at least he tries. "Hmm, let's see, we need someone who can get a bunch of kids to come to a dance. Well, we have someone who got an actual *celebrity* to come to her taco truck. And who was that? Here's a hint, Julia, not *you*."

It was nice of Arthur to try to help, but even I have to admit, that's more than a stretch. Maybe I'd never say so out loud, but I didn't even recognize Viviana Vega when she was standing right in front of me. "That's okay, Arthur," I tell him. "Julia can be in charge of publicity. I'll make the posters. That's all I really wanted to do anyway."

Our planning hour is almost up, and Mr. Salazar, who had retreated to his desk, finally intervenes. "All right." He claps his hands. "Sounds like you've laid some good groundwork. Next time, you better dig into some *actual* work."

And we do.

Amanda gets excused from soccer practice the next week

so she can join us in the studio. She brings along an armful of leftover gift wrap and instructions for folding the paper into big origami stars. "We'll string a bunch together and hang them from the ceiling," she explains before she and the rest of the decorations team take over one of the art tables to start cutting and creasing.

Meanwhile, the refreshments team drafts a letter to the grocery store, asking the manager if he'll consider donating soda and ice cream for us to sell at the dance. Mami has promised to deliver the letter as soon as it's ready.

Julia and I float among the groups. When we decide everything is under control, she joins Maddie, who is making a list of nearby schools to invite. I grab a scratch pad and sit down next to Arthur, who is working on his playlist. I know I need to get started on those posters, but I'm not feeling very inspired. Arthur had found an article in one of his magazines filled with images of vintage concert posters and lent it to me this morning. I retrieve the magazine from my backpack and start flipping through the pages, hoping one of them will spark an idea.

When nothing comes to mind, I decide to take Ms. Barlow's advice and just start. Arthur pulls his headphones down and looks over my shoulder. "It's good," he says. Polite, but not enthusiastic. And he's right.

"Yeah. But it's not exactly what we need."

He slides the headphones back on. "Nope."

Mr. Salazar walks over as I'm tapping my pencil on the paper.

"Stuck?"

"A little."

"Remember," he says, "you're leading this committee because you care about art. So tell me, why does art matter?" He puts a hand over his heart. "To *you*—why does it matter?"

I close my eyes to think about it for a second. "To me? I guess because... well, when I can't think of what to say or how to explain the way I feel... I can... usually... draw it?" Mr. Salazar nods and walks away, and the seed of a new idea begins to grow.

When it's time to go home, I put away my sketches and collect my backpack. Before I leave, I overhear Maddie and Julia talking as they clean up their work area.

"But I just don't get why Arthur is wasting time on a playlist when Stef is going to get Viviana Vega to come. She, like, knows her now or something."

"She doesn't know her," Julia fumes. "She sold her a *Bur.Eat.Oh.*" The syllables sound like rubber bands snapping, one after the other.

Quickly, I close the door behind me. Maddie can't be serious, can she? I thought all of that Viviana Vega talk had blown over. My hand is closed around the doorknob. I'm about to turn it, to go back in and correct her. But I change my mind and let go. Maddie would know I'd been eavesdropping, I reason. And anyway, if people are going to whisper behind my back, having them say I'm friends with a pop star isn't exactly the worst rumor in the world. Plus, if I look at it one way—really squint at it—I *could* say I know Viviana Vega. Sort of. I know her better than anyone else in our school, that's for sure, and definitely better than Julia.

CHAPTER
22

But by the end of the week, what started as a crazy rumor has spread like sniffles during cold season. It hasn't gotten any less crazy, but everyone seems to believe it's true, and I'm worried I can't ignore it much longer. Eighth graders who've never even looked at me in the hallways are waiting for me at my locker to ask if Viviana Vega is really coming to our gym. Sixth graders are tapping me shyly on the shoulder and begging for autographs. I don't know what to say, so mostly, I don't say anything. I just shrug. "Oh, you know," I answer. "We'll see." Not exactly a yes, but not exactly a no.

"So you'll never guess," Amanda begins, slamming her

lunch tray on the table on Friday afternoon, "what Trish asked me at soccer practice yesterday."

"Geez, easy," Arthur complains.

"Sorry," she says. "Anyway, she asked me to ask *you* if she could take a picture with *Viviana Vega* at the big art dance. Crazy, right?"

"Yeah. Crazy." I peel the tinfoil wrapping from one of Papi's homemade chicken-and-corn burritos—somehow they taste even better a day old—and try to sound nonchalant. "What did you tell her?"

Before Amanda can answer, two eighth graders plop down on the bench across from me at the table. "Can you get Viviana to dedicate a song to me?" one of them interrupts. "Any song. Just ask her, okay?"

I give my usual shrug and point to my mouth like it's so full of burrito I can't possibly say a word. "Humm...mmh."

Amanda and Arthur stop chewing. They stare at me with their mouths hanging open while I kick them under the table, hoping they get the message: *Please, don't say anything.* Finally, the eighth graders seem satisfied and walk away.

Amanda and Arthur are still staring at me when I swallow.

"What?" I ask, taking a sip from my water bottle.

"*What?* You're taking dedications now?" Arthur asks sarcastically.

"Well...I...you know...anyway, this is *so* your fault," I

sputter. "If you hadn't opened your mouth in art class, nobody would be expecting me to bring Viviana Vega to school."

"*My* fault?" Arthur looks as though I'd just slapped him. His cheeks even turn a little pink. "I was trying to stick up for you, and I *never* said you were going to bring Viviana Vega."

Amanda, quietly for once, says, "They believe that because you let them."

Part of me knows they're right; part of me is trying to gulp down a big lump of embarrassment. But another part of me is stung to hear my best friends call me out, right in the middle of the cafeteria.

"I don't believe this," I say, shaking my head. "You two just can't stand that I'm the one finally getting some attention, can you?"

Neither of them answers. Arthur pulls on his headphones. He leans his head on one arm while lazily pushing carrot sticks around his plate. Amanda stares at her tray for a couple of minutes before stuffing the apple in her pocket and getting up to leave. We don't talk for the rest of the afternoon, and it feels so much worse than driving home in Tía Perla ever did.

CHAPTER
23

After Mami and I help with the shopping at the farmers' market and the prep work at the commissary on Saturday morning, Papi drives home and pulls over at the curb in front of our house to drop us off. Mami hops out and holds the door open for me, but instead of following her, I ask if I can spend the day with Papi and Tía Perla. My parents look a little surprised, but they agree. Mami blows kisses from the porch as we drive away.

"Can we start at the park?" I ask. Amanda will be there, and I have to talk to her, face-to-face, before the awkward silence between us drifts into another school week.

"Por qué no?" Papi agrees.

We get to the park as parents are staking out spots on the sidelines with beach chairs and big umbrellas. Some of the teams have already started warming up. After a while, I see Amanda jump out of her mom's car, a gym bag slung over her shoulder. She runs over to where her team is practicing and flops down on the grass to put on her cleats. Even if she wanted to, she won't have time to talk to me until after her game is over, so I decide to help Papi with Tía Perla.

He slides into a smooth, easy rhythm when he cooks, almost like he's dancing to one of his banda songs. Only there isn't any music playing—just Papi's happy hum as he does something he loves and has worked hard for. As the fields scramble to life with the morning's earliest games, Tía Perla's kitchen starts sizzling with the morning's first orders. I call each one back to Papi. With a quick nod of his head, he drops a lump of butter onto the grill and waits for it to melt into a shimmering, yellow puddle. He adds chicken or beef, then bell peppers and cilantro. As the meat cooks, steam rises, braiding the smells of peppers, onions, and nose-tickling spices, before they escape through Tía Perla's blue-tinted vents. It is the first burrito of the day that sells all the others, Papi always tells me, beckoning new customers with its warm, tempting aroma.

When the meat is nearly cooked, Papi peels one or two tortillas from a stack inside Tía Perla's refrigerator and presses them to the grill with his gloved hand—only a few seconds on each side, just long enough to make the tortillas soft. Then he piles the meat inside and adds a ladleful of salsa. After crumbling salty cotija cheese over the top, he folds the burrito tightly in one fluid motion, then puts the whole thing back on the grill, lightly toasting the tortilla to give it a little crunch. Finally, he wraps the burrito in paper before handing it off to me to drop into a bag and hand to the customer whose mouth, by this time, is usually watering.

Lunchtime is when Papi's dance is trickiest but also most graceful as he pivots from grill to fridge to sink to cupboard, never missing a beat and never mixing up an order.

Lately, though, the nagging buzz of his cell phone breaks his rhythm. When other drivers call to talk taco truck strategy, Papi pins his phone between his ear and his shoulder while he stirs the meat over the grill. I hear snippets of his conversations as I listen for the long whistle that means Amanda's game is over.

To me, all the phone calls sound the same. They start with Papi shaking his head as he says again and again that it isn't fair, that they have to fight. Before long, the maybes begin: "Maybe if we…maybe if they…maybe if I…" until Papi finally says sadly, "Whatever happens, happens."

That's when I want to take the phone out of his hands and say, "No. No, you can't just let things happen." That's how I got into this Viviana Vega mess, and now I have to *do* something. But first, I need Arthur and Amanda back on my side. The whistle blows. Her game ends. The teams start shaking hands.

I know I can't count on Amanda to come looking for me after what happened at lunch on Friday, so I take a bottle of soda from the fridge and ask Papi if I can run over to say hello. He crouches down and peers out the order window as if trying to size up the distance between us and Amanda.

"I'll have my phone," I remind him, patting my pocket.

That seems to satisfy him. He stands upright again and waves me off.

CHAPTER 24

I hang back, leaning against a tree, and wait until Amanda is done talking with her teammates before I approach her. "Hey," I say, holding the cherry soda out in front of me.

"No, thanks," she says when she sees it. Her face is bright red. I know it's from the game, but it makes her look really angry, and part of me wants to turn around and walk back to Tía Perla.

But I take a deep breath and pull back the soda. "Okay. I just wanted to say I'm sorry about yesterday. It's my fault the Viviana Vega rumor got out of hand, and I shouldn't have taken it out on you and Arthur."

Amanda narrows her eyes at me, smiles, then holds out her hand for the soda. "Okay."

I finally exhale, and we sit down on the grass.

"I really need your help," I tell her, pulling tiny leaves off sprigs of clover. "We have to figure out what to do about this."

"Help with what? Just tell everyone she's not coming. They'll be mad. Then they'll get over it."

I've thought of that, but there has to be some other way. A way to get Viviana Vega to come to Saint Scholastica. It sounds impossible, but the idea that a celebrity would come to Tía Perla's order window sounded impossible once, too. When I explain it to Amanda, she groans and throws herself back on the grass. I'm bracing myself for another argument when she says, "Fine."

"Fine?"

"Fine," she repeats, sitting up. "We'll think of something. But you better tell Arthur you're sorry. We need him, too."

Amanda sees her mom waving at her from the field where her younger brother's game just ended. She gets up and dusts the grass off her shorts, saying, "I still think you should just tell the truth and get it over with."

I roll my eyes.

"They'll get stuck up there," she calls over her shoulder.

I feel a million times better when I get back to Tía Perla. In the time it's taken me to smooth things over with Amanda, another truck has pulled up, Taquizas La Paloma. When Papi isn't on the phone with other drivers, he's meeting them in person to worry or plot or complain. But I don't have time to wonder which they're doing now. I go into the cab and rifle through the glove box for a pen and something to write on. I find an old envelope—that should work—and take it over to the card table that Papi has set up for our customers. Then I sit clicking my pen—open, close, open, close—trying to think up a plan.

Before I know it, twenty minutes have passed. And instead of even one good idea, all I have are a dozen little doodles crammed into a corner of the envelope. I crumple it up and start rubbing my temples.

I hear Papi call, "Adios!" as the other truck driver pulls away. Then, instead of getting back inside the truck, he sits down next to me at the card table. "I need your help with something."

The drivers are all preparing their speeches for the big city council meeting, Papi explains. He wants to write one, too. "It needs to be very professional," he says. "No mistakes." I can see he doesn't trust his English enough to write the speech on his own. I know he's asking me to write it for him—and I know how embarrassing that must be.

But still. I have my own problems right now, and I don't really feel like letting Tía Perla stand in my way again. I look away.

"It's just that I'm pretty busy right now," I tell him. "With . . . school stuff. And the dance and everything . . ." My voice trails off. Papi doesn't say anything. He just pats my hand, stands up, and walks back to the truck. A little well of guilt bubbles up in my throat, but just like missing the concert, maybe this is for the best. It's time to get back to brainstorming. I turn over the envelope to make a fresh start.

The rest of the afternoon is so busy at the park that Papi says we can call it quits and head back to the commissary early. With the city council meeting just two days away, the place crackles with nervous anticipation like drops of water on a sizzling pan. Someone has written SAVE OUR TRUCKS! across the meeting notice. Drivers huddle over highlighted printouts of the proposed regulations, fine-tuning their arguments.

Papi shakes their hands as he leaves the commissary. They wish one another good luck and agree to meet outside city hall on Monday night so they can walk in as a group.

"Remember to put on a clean shirt," one of the drivers jokes, nudging Papi in the ribs. "You're going to be on TV."

I wait until we're in the pickup to ask Papi what he meant.

"It's not like real TV," Papi explains. "They tape the meetings and show them on the public-access channel so people who can't be there in person can still follow along. I don't think anyone really watches it, though."

I'm relieved. I know how nervous Papi gets when he has to speak English in front of strangers. Just the thought of him having to speak English on *television* was making me nervous, too. And now I understand why he wanted my help.

So on Sunday night, when he asks to rehearse his speech,

I switch off the TV, put down the laundry, and really try to listen. Reading off index cards, he talks about hard work and supporting a family and raising a daughter. He looks up, unsure, at Mami and me. She nods encouragingly, and he continues. He talks about opportunity and the American dream, and for the first time in a long time, I remember that sweet, strawberry-soda feeling when Tía Perla was a dream all three of us shared.

CHAPTER
25

No one is waiting for me outside the classroom when I get to school on Monday morning. I'm not surprised, but the knots in my stomach tighten anyway. Amanda is at her desk, finishing last night's homework. She looks up when she sees me, and I bite my lip. She rolls her eyes and nods toward Arthur. *Just* do *it*, she mouths.

Amanda had let me off pretty easily at the park—all it took was an apology and a soda. But she never stays mad very long. Amanda boils over and cools right back down. Arthur's different. His anger is more like a slow, steady simmer, especially when someone has hurt his feelings. And I've known him long enough to know I did.

He's in his seat, headphones on under a thick hooded sweatshirt that he's wearing even though it's not even close to cold outside. I stand in front of his desk for a few seconds, waiting for him to look up. When he doesn't, I say, "Arthur?"

Nothing.

"*Arthur,*" I try again, louder. "Arthur, I'm trying to apologize."

I know he can hear me, but he barely blinks.

"Hey!" I bark, pulling his hood down around his neck. His hair underneath is a crazy mess of just-out-of-bed spikes.

"Hey, your*self* !" he shoots back, finally taking off his headphones. "You're supposed to be apologizing, remember?"

Right. "Sorry."

"Well?"

"Well, I'm sorry. I'm really sorry. I was a jerk. Do you forgive me?"

He shrugs, and the headphones go back on. "I'll think about it." But I've known him long enough to know he already has.

It's a good thing, too, because by now it seems like Julia is the only one—besides Arthur and Amanda, of course—who isn't expecting Viviana Vega to show up at our school.

"You know she isn't coming." Julia is seething on the way into the art studio for our dance-planning session after school. "Why do you keep pretending she is?"

"Well, she won't if we don't even *try*," I answer. But I know

I have to think of something fast, and I'm counting on my friends for help.

Julia blinks. "Whatever." She pulls a binder labeled DANCE out of her backpack and finds our master checklist. Almost every box is ticked. Amanda and her team have folded hundreds of paper stars and strung them together in long, shiny garlands. The grocery store has promised the refreshments team not just ice cream and soda but plates and napkins as well. Arthur has turned his playlist over to Mr. Salazar for approval, and Maddie has sent invitations to all the middle schools nearby.

And, finally, I have something to contribute, too, something more than half-truths and exaggerations.

I wait for Julia to get to "posters" on our checklist. Just as I expected, she puts her hands on her hips and taps her foot impatiently. "Well, Stef? How much longer are we going to have to wait?"

"Oh, about two more seconds," I say, opening Mr. Salazar's supply closet and pulling out the poster I stashed there earlier. I unroll it then and hold it up for everyone to see.

"Whoa," Jake whispers.

"Nice," says Arthur. Even Julia and Maddie look impressed.

Inspired by the Viviana Vega poster Arthur had given me, mine shows dozens of arms, painted in gray and black and white, all reaching upward. But instead of reaching toward Viviana—they're holding up paintbrushes and pencils, pastels and palettes. I wrote FEEL THE HEARTBEAT across the top, the "art" in "heart" drawn in bold red strokes.

"Very well done," Mr. Salazar says as my poster is passed around the room. He promises to make copies and have them ready for us to tape all over school tomorrow.

CHAPTER
26

I'm perplexed to see the pickup in the parking lot instead of Tía Perla that afternoon.

"What's going on?" I ask Papi as I toss my backpack into the truck bed. "Are we picking up Tía Perla from here?"

"No, m'ija. Remember? Tonight is the city council meeting. We're not taking Tía Perla out."

That's right. I nod and look out the window. It's a warm afternoon. The days have started getting longer but not yet hot. If Papi had been working, it would be the perfect kind of evening to take Tía Perla to a park. Neighbors would be walking their dogs. Moms and dads would be tossing Frisbees to sons and daughters. Soccer teams would be dribbling their balls around orange cones. They would all see Tía Perla and realize they were craving tacos.

I had even come up with a name for this kind of evening: Taco Weather. It was a code phrase between Papi and me. "Looks like Taco Weather," one of us would say, and both of us knew it would be a busy, beautiful night. I don't mention it today, though. Both of us have more serious things on our minds.

"Mami took the night off," Papi tells me, "and you can stay home with her if you want. I know you have a lot of work to do. But I had hoped . . . well, I thought we might all go to the meeting together."

I imagine myself sitting in an uncomfortable chair in a crowded room while a bunch of food truck drivers talk to a bunch of men and women in suits about a bunch of rules that don't have anything to do with me.

"What for?"

"Well, m'ija, I know what I want to say. But it's really important that I say it right. No mistakes. The other drivers are counting on me—we're all counting on one another— and I think the city council will understand much better what I'm trying to say if *you* say it. Will you come with me and read the speech?"

He has to be kidding. Didn't he say this meeting was going to be on television? I mean, I know what it's like to have something important to say and feel like *nobody* can understand you, but this is too much. I can't do it. I look at my shoes.

"Can we just go home?" I mumble. "I'm sorry. I just want to go home. I have school stuff, and I need to call Amanda, and I don't think I would be any good up there."

"Órale," he says, patting my knee. "Don't be sorry. You and your mami can watch us from home."

Mami meets us at the door and hustles us into the kitchen, where dinner is already prepared "Siéntense and eat up," she says. "We need to get out of here quickly if we want to find three seats together."

I cringe, and Papi intervenes.

"Maybe it would be better if you and Estefania stay home after all," he says. "She has a lot of studying to do."

Mami looks at me, then back at Papi, and seems uncertain. "Well, you need to eat anyway," she says. "Sit down."

Papi serves himself two enchiladas dripping with red sauce. But once they're on his plate, he only picks at them. He pulls his note cards out of his pocket, and I watch his lips move softly as he reads his speech to himself.

Meanwhile, Mami paces the kitchen, carrying a glass of water from the counter to the table, and then back to the counter again. She says over and over—to Papi? To me? To herself? I'm not sure—"It's going to be fine. Just wait. It's going to be fine." She's not eating, either, and I don't have much of an appetite myself.

"Can I be excused?" Without waiting for an answer, I grab the cordless phone off its cradle and take it to my bedroom. As I dial Amanda's house, I hear Mami kiss Papi's forehead and wish him luck. The front door closes behind him, and he drives off for the meeting.

Amanda picks up on the third ring. We talk about the essays we have to turn in to Ms. Barlow and the mystery smell in Mrs. Serros's room before I get down to business. "I still don't know what to do about Viviana Vega. Have you thought of anything?"

"You mean, besides the truth?" she asks.

"Ha. Ha."

"Well, what about an impersonator, then?"

"Know any?"

"Can't you pull it off?"

I hear footsteps in the hallway and then a knock at my bedroom door.

"Estefania?" Mami says through the crack. "The meeting has started."

I tell Amanda I have to go, then join Mami on the living room sofa.

CHAPTER
27

On the screen, I see three men and two women sitting in leather swivel chairs behind a massive table. Each is wearing a suit jacket, and each has been poured a tall glass of water. Facing the table is a wooden podium, and behind that are rows and rows of folding chairs. Every seat is filled. I can't see any of the faces in the audience, only the backs of their heads. Knowing that Papi is in one of those chairs—that sometime tonight he'll get up and speak at that podium—sets a million butterflies aflutter in my stomach. Mami takes my hand.

The woman at the center of the table, wearing an ivory blazer and peering down through reading glasses, lightly taps her gavel. "Let's move on to Agenda Item 4: Proposed Regulations for Mobile Food Vendors."

The man sitting next to her clears his throat. "Mayor Barnhart, I am presenting these proposals at the request of some concerned citizens who are worried about health and safety risks associated with the growing number of food trucks in our community. I'd like to open this up to public debate."

Mayor Barnhart looks out into the audience. "It looks like we might have some public comment?" A line forms at the podium, long and wriggly.

A woman with short brown hair and a long gauzy scarf goes first. She bends the microphone so that it's closer to her mouth, takes a quick look behind her, and speaks.

Her family owns a diner in town, she says. It has been in her family for decades. But now, all the food trucks parked nearby are stealing her customers. It's not fair, she complains. Trucks don't have to pay for bathrooms or buildings, carpets or air-conditioning. "Please pass these regulations to level the playing field again." The men and women at the table take notes. Some nod their heads. I look at Mami, and she's biting her lip. We scoot closer together on the couch.

Next at the podium is a man in a blue-striped shirt with rolled-up sleeves. He says he lives near a park where taco trucks come every weekend. "Some of these things are so old and unsightly you just have to wonder about cleanliness, you know? And what about air pollution? What about the noise? What if a truck were to hit one of the kids?"

A few people in the audience clap. The man in the striped shirt goes back to his seat, and a man in a green sweater takes his place at the podium. He tells the city council he owns a bakery and coffee shop. His wife, he says, got sick after eating at a taco truck not too long ago. "If that happened at my shop, the health inspectors would be all over me. These trucks need to abide by the same rules as the rest of us!" He pounds the podium with his fist. It makes a dull thud—the same sound as my heart falling when I think about where this meeting is headed.

I have my complaints about Tía Perla, but I can't bear listening to these strangers anymore. It feels like they're picking on a friend, and suddenly I can't believe I'm not there to stick up for her.

"Mami, we have to go," I say, jumping off the couch.

"M'ija, I know it's hard to watch right now, but let's see what happens. Your papi hasn't even had his turn yet."

I'm already in my bedroom, pulling my shoes back on. "No, Mami. I mean, let's go!" I call to her. "We should be there. With Papi."

I'm back in the living room seconds later. Mami stares at me, momentarily shocked. Then she looks at the television and at her keys on the coffee table. "Órale."

CHAPTER
28

Mami drops me off in front of the city hall steps. I scramble up, two at a time, while she finds a place to park. On the frantic ride over, I had come up with a plan: Find Papi and read his speech, just like he asked. But when I open the doors, I realize it's impossible. I have to tap on shoulders—"Excuse me"—and squeeze between elbows—"Sorry, can I get by?"— just to shove my way inside. I search the crowd for familiar faces. I see a few, but I don't see Papi.

Then, all of a sudden, I hear him. "Good evening. My name is Samuel Soto."

Somehow, his voice through the microphone sounds

thinner and smaller than it does in our kitchen. "I thank you for your time tonight."

He stops. Clears his throat.

"Five years ago, I bought my food truck. It isn't much, but it is my dream, my family's American dream."

I *have* to get to the podium. I step on toes; I jostle handbags; I almost fall into someone's lap as I scramble to the front of the room.

Papi continues. "My wife and I, we came to this country prepared to work hard because we believed the promise: that if we worked hard, we could build a new life, support a family."

By now, I'm close enough to see him. He shuffles his note cards, looks up at the city council, then back down at his hands. "And it's true." He nods. "We have sweat, and we have saved. With hard work, we have built a life we can be proud of. But if you pass these new rules, all that work will go to waste. If we have to move our trucks every hour, we'll spend more money on gas than we earn selling burritos. And when it comes to public restrooms, well, doesn't it make more sense for me to park where I can find customers rather than where I can find a toilet?"

A couple of the council members chuckle. Papi looks up and smiles. He seems steadier now, the version of himself that confidently commands Tía Perla's kitchen.

"My friends and I pay taxes," he goes on. "Some of us have even hired employees. What happens to those jobs if we go out of business?"

His voice drops again. "Now, as for me and my family, our little truck will never make us rich. But I am happy just to raise my daughter and give her an education. Give her better chances than I had so maybe she won't have to work so very hard."

He shrugs and tucks the note cards in his shirt pocket. "That's all. We don't want special treatment. Just a fair chance."

Finally, I'm standing right behind him. He hears me and turns around. "Qué pasó?" he whispers. I wave at him to keep going.

He turns back to the city council and hurriedly finishes. "Once again, thank you for your time."

The mayor lifts her gavel. "Hearing no further comment, I call for a vote. All those in favor—"

"Wait!"

Is that really my voice? Still echoing in my ears, it sounds like someone else's. I have no idea what I'm doing, but I can't let this vote happen. Not yet.

The mayor still has her gavel raised. "Yes?"

I look over my shoulder, where rows and rows of people are quietly and curiously staring at me. I gulp.

"Young lady, is there something I can do for you? We really do need to move on."

I swallow. "Yes, please. If it's not too late, there's something I'd like to say."

I hear sighs behind me. One of the men at the table looks at his watch. Mayor Barnhart sets down her gavel. "I suppose there's enough time for one more comment," she says. "Go ahead. But please go quickly."

I turn to Papi, who looks down at me, both eyebrows raised like two dark question marks. I nod to him, and he whispers, "Órale," then bends the microphone low enough for me to speak into it. Finally, he steps away from the podium.

"Please state your name for the record," Mayor Barnhart says.

"My name is Stef Soto. Estefania Soto." Now what?

I look up at the city council—watching me.

Back at the audience—watching me.

Over at Papi—watching me, too.

"If you have something to add," the mayor says impatiently, "please get on with it."

I remember what Ms. Barlow told me. Just start somewhere. So I take a deep breath and start.

"Tía Perla isn't really my aunt. That's just what we call our taco truck," I begin. There is laughter behind me. My face feels hot—red fireworks exploding across my cheeks. But then I remember Mr. Salazar pressing me to explain what matters to *me*, and I keep going.

"I'm not sure I even like her, but I know she matters. To

me. She's *our* truck. We all worked really hard for her; we still work hard for her. And she works hard for us. My papi always obeys the rules. Sometimes I think he likes rules a little *too* much."

That gets another laugh.

"It's like he said, he doesn't want special treatment, just to be treated fairly. So I hope you'll reconsider. Because even though Tía Perla isn't really my aunt, she *is* sort of like family."

Half the room applauds.

Papi puts his hand on my shoulder and leads me back to his seat. As we walk past, drivers reach out to squeeze my hand, whispering "Good job, m'ija" and "Well done." I smile and take Papi's seat. He leans down and says, "Thank you," then stands up next to me.

The mayor taps her gavel. "Now that public comments are *really* finished, I think it's finally time for a vote. In the interest of fairness, let's take these proposals one by one. First, the proposal requiring food trucks to move locations every sixty minutes—all those in favor, please say aye." No one says a thing. "Any opposed, say nay." All five of them say nay.

It didn't pass. A small cheer rises among the drivers. One down. I look up at Papi hopefully. He smiles and takes my hand.

They move on to the next proposal. Must food trucks be required to park within one hundred feet of a public restroom?

No again.

We all cheer—a little louder this time.

"And finally," says the mayor, "the proposal requiring mobile vending permits to be renewed annually, instead of every five years, and to be granted based, in part, on vehicle appearance. All those in favor?"

One of the councilmen leans into the microphone. "Well," he says, "the first two proposals did seem unfair and unnecessary. But I think we can all agree we don't want a bunch of mobile eyesores roaming our city. I'm voting in favor of the measure."

"Aye," says the councilman sitting next to him, nodding his head.

The others follow—"Aye" and "Aye"—and then the mayor speaks again, "I see no reason why mobile food vendors *shouldn't* keep their trucks clean and well maintained. It's unanimous." She strikes the table with her gavel.

I look at the drivers in the audience, some whispering to one another, others shrugging their shoulders. Two out of three isn't bad. They seem to be agreeing. I tug at Papi's shirt-sleeve, wanting to congratulate him. He looks down at me and smiles but keeps his arms folded across his chest.

After Mayor Barnhart hammers down her gavel one last time to close the meeting, the audience really erupts, cheering and shaking hands. I jump out of my seat, too, swept up in the excitement. As Papi and I walk out together, we spot Mami waiting at the back of the room, clapping and smiling at us.

She tousles my hair and, kissing my forehead, says, "M'ija, I am so proud. You did it."

The other drivers are planning to meet up at the commissary to celebrate. I tell Mami to go on ahead, that I want to ride with Papi.

"You can ride with me, Estefania," he says. "But I don't think we'll go to the commissary. Let's just go home. It's been a long night." His voice is tired and quiet again, and I can't understand it. Haven't we just won? Aren't we happy? Isn't this exactly what we wanted? I study his face for clues but don't find any.

"Okay," I say. "Let's go home, then."

CHAPTER
29

We had been out so late the night before that Mami and Papi let me sleep in the next morning. Mami drops me off at school with a note excusing my tardiness, and after checking in at the office, I walk down the long, empty hallway to Ms. Barlow's classroom, pausing at the door. There's no way anyone would have seen me on public access last night, right?

But if anyone saw the meeting, they don't mention it—no one looks up from their reading as I slide quietly into my seat.

"Stef, would you come up and see me for just a sec?" It's Ms. Barlow. She'll want to know why I didn't get to class on time.

"I'm really sorry," I start to say. "It's just, we were out really late, and—"

She puts a hand up to stop me. "I know why you were out late. I always watch the city council meetings on TV."

Oh no. She's not going to make a big deal of this, is she?

"Don't worry. I'm not going to make a big deal of this. I just wanted to tell you that you should be proud. You're quite persuasive when you speak from your gut."

That gives me an idea.

I have to wait until lunchtime to tell Arthur and Amanda.

When she hears it, Amanda wrinkles her nose. "*That's* your big idea?"

I know it's not much. But for some reason, I think it might work.

I decide to write a letter to Viviana Vega. I'll show her how much art means to us. I'll tell her how much we need her help. "You know, from the gut," I say as I finish explaining.

Viviana's an artist, too. I think she'll get it.

"I guess it could work," Amanda says. She looks doubt-ful. "But where are you going to send it? She didn't write her address on that fifty-dollar bill, did she?"

Good point. I bang my head against the lunch table.

"Relax, drama queen," Arthur says. "You can send it to her record label."

"Her record label?"

"The company that puts out her music," he says. "You write the letter; I'll find the address."

Arthur comes through, and the next morning, he passes me a scrap of paper. His handwriting is scratchy and scribbly, but I can make out the address.

"You did it!" I say, a little too loudly. Ms. Barlow looks at us suspiciously over the top of her yogurt cup.

This is perfect. I could hug Arthur and almost do, but just as I'm about to throw my arms around his neck, he slips his headphones—and his hood—over his ears again. I go back to my desk to reread my letter in the few minutes before school starts.

Dear Ms. Vega,

My name is Stef Soto. You probably don't remember me, but I sold you a burrito not too long ago. Wheat-free, dairy-free, egg-free, nut-free, meat-free. I hope you liked it.

I'm writing to you because the art program at my school, Saint Scholastica, needs help. We're almost completely out of art supplies. My art class is holding a dance to raise money to buy some, but we could raise a lot more if you were there.

I'm not always very good at explaining how I feel or what I think. But art helps me find my voice. As a singer, I'm sure you'll understand.

I stop and think before adding one more line:

If you come, I'll make sure my papi has a dozen of those special burritos for you.

Sincerely,
Stef Soto

That afternoon, on the way to meet up with Papi at the gas station, I drop the letter into a blue mailbox. "Please, please, please, please, *please* let this work," I whisper as the letter falls. After that, the only thing left to do is wait.

Every day, after Papi and I get home from the commissary, I check the mail for a letter from Viviana Vega. Every day, I find nothing but fast-food coupons and furniture ads.

CHAPTER
30

Tía Perla hasn't picked me up from school since before the big city council meeting, so it's a surprise—and not necessarily an unpleasant one—to hear the *chirp chirp chirp* of her horn after school.

"See you guys." I wave to Arthur and Amanda. I start walking over to Papi and then stop, right in the middle of the parking lot. Parents honk and swerve around me, but for a moment, I can't move. Taped inside Tía Perla's passenger-side window is a sign: FOR SALE.

I don't know what to say as I open the door, so I just throw down my backpack and buckle my seat belt, trying to figure out what Papi could possibly be thinking.

"I mean, is this a joke?" I burst out after we're a mile or so away. "After all those phone calls? The speeches? The city council? After we *won*? What was the point? Does Mami even know?"

Papi pulls over, squeezes the steering wheel with both hands, and turns to me. He spoke to Mami last night, he tells me, after I went to bed. She understands.

"You've seen all those brand-new food trucks at the commissary, m'ija," he says.

I think about the newer trucks I've seen in the lot: Tip Top Tapas, Bánh Mì Oh My, Chai Chai Again. Gleaming chrome and sparkling paint.

"You know I love Tía Perla, but even I have to admit, she's looking pretty run-down, no? It's hard enough finding customers, and I don't think we can compete much longer." He shakes his head. "No. I'll go back to painting, and maybe someday we'll save enough for another truck—maybe a real restaurant this time."

It still doesn't make sense. "Then why did we work so hard—why did we get up and speak in front of all those people if we were just going to quit?" For months, I've been wishing Tía Perla would just roll out of my life, but now that it's happening, I want to slam on the brakes.

"We did it," Papi says simply, "because our compadres needed us." He glances in the rearview mirror then and steers us back onto the road. "Now. How about we take the night off? Suzy's?"

Papi talks nonstop through dinner—about the dance, about his plans for the garden, about Mami's promotion. About everything but the taco truck. I try to listen. I try to mirror his smiles. I try to enjoy the food at least, but it all tastes bland.

Back at home, I sit on the couch with the stack of today's mail and switch on the lamp, not really expecting to find anything.

Bill. Bill. Magazine. Credit card application. I sigh and put the stack on the coffee table, where Mami and Papi can sift through it later. Then I notice an envelope on the floor.

It's addressed to me. I must have dropped it.

I jump to my feet. My heart thumps in my ears, and my palms begin to sweat as I hold the envelope in both hands, suddenly unsure if I should open it. This is it: the moment that decides whether I'm Stef Soto, Taco Queen, or Stef Soto, seventh-grade hero.

I tear the envelope open. The first thing I pull out is a black-and-white photo of Viviana Vega. In the corner of the picture is a note scrawled in silver ink: "Thanks for listening, Stef!" Underneath is a swoosh of letters I can't really read—I guess it's her signature.

I don't know what to make of it. There's nothing about my letter, nothing about the dance. I check the envelope again.

This looks more promising. I pull out a piece of paper, folded in half. Quickly, I unfold it, and my eyes race over the typed page.

Dear Miss Soto,

Thanks for taking the time to write to Viviana Vega! She loves to hear from fans like you! Stay in touch with Viviana by joining the Viviana Vega fan club. For a one-time membership fee, you'll receive regular updates from Viviana, whether she's on the road or in the studio! You'll always be the first to know!

So many exclamation points and so little help.

I've been holding my breath, and after reading the note, it rushes out of me like air from a popped balloon. She isn't coming. And worse than that, she hadn't even read my letter, probably hadn't even seen it. I sink back into the couch and hold my still-pounding head in my hands. Now what?

CHAPTER
31

The next morning, Ms. Barlow writes our journal exercise on the whiteboard: YOU WAKE UP AND REALIZE YOU'RE INVISIBLE. WHAT DO YOU DO?

That's easy: Celebrate.

"Just tell everyone the truth," Amanda says when I show her and Arthur the letter. Arthur asks for the autographed photo to keep as part of his pop music memorabilia collection. Fine with me.

"Amanda's right." Arthur nods. "I mean, it's not really that big of a deal. I'm sure no one actually thought she was coming. They're just glad we're having a dance."

After school in the art studio, Mr. Salazar asks for final

reports from all the team captains. The refreshments team has twelve dozen ice cream cups stored in the cafeteria freezer, plus six cases of bottled water and another six of soda.

"Bravo," Mr. Salazar says. He claps a few times slowly, and the whole class joins him in the applause.

The publicity team has hung my posters in all the bathrooms and hallways. Some of the teachers even taped them up in their classrooms. And tomorrow, during morning announcements, Maddie will remind all the middle schoolers to come to the dance. Another round of applause.

Amanda stands up next, reporting that her team will begin decorating the cafeteria after lunch tomorrow.

Mr. Salazar thanks her. "Congratulations. It's sounding as if this project is going to be a resounding success."

It also sounds like Mr. Salazar might skip right over me. Until Christopher interrupts him. "Wait, what about Viviana Vega?"

Suddenly, the whole class is looking at me—Mr. Salazar confused, but the rest of them eager.

"Everything's going great," I mumble into my lap.

Amanda kicks me under the table. Arthur opens his eyes wide, as though he's trying to make me tell the truth by mind control.

Fine. Just get it over with. "She's not coming."

Silence.

Not knowing what else to do, Arthur and Amanda start

clapping—but they aren't loud enough to overpower the disappointed groans that roll through the studio. It's Julia, of all people, who quiets everyone down. "Guys, seriously. *Noooo*body thought Stef was really going to get Viviana Vega to come to the dance."

I don't know if I'm offended or relieved.

"*So*," she continues. "I talked to my parents, and they're going to pay for a DJ! Like, a real one. It's going to be a*maz*-ing." She sparkles, as usual.

Then, even without Mr. Salazar's help, there's an explosion of applause.

"What about Arthur's playlist?" I protest. He's slumped on his stool, his hood pulled halfway down over his face.

But no one listens to me. Julia is the center of attention again, and I'm the girl most likely to smell like taco sauce. When Mr. Salazar says it's time to go, I pick up my things without looking back—without even saying good-bye to Arthur and Amanda. I speed-walk through the parking lot.

CHAPTER
32

I call Amanda from my cell phone right after I've finished my homework. This counts as urgent.

"So how bad is it?" I demand.

"Oh, *hiiii*," she gushes with sarcastic sweetness. "I'm just *fiiiine*. Thank you so much for *aaaasking*."

Point taken. "Okay, okay, I'm sorry. But please, just tell me. What were they saying after I left?"

"I don't know." She yawns. "Not a lot. I guess some people are kind of annoyed with you. But everyone thinks the DJ thing is cool. Except Arthur, obviously."

I'm not convinced.

Mami and Papi won't let me stay home from school on

Friday, but they can't make me go to the dance. Not even Arthur and Amanda change my mind. They try all day, but there's no way I'm going.

"Come on," Arthur nags one last time as he's stepping into his mom's car. "If I can go, you can go. I bet everyone's already starting to forget the whole Viviana Vega thing."

Well, I'm not about to remind them.

I find Tía Perla waiting for me in her old spot at the far end of the parking lot—maybe for the last time, I think. Papi is leaning out his rolled-down window, talking to a woman in a knee-length skirt and pointy black shoes. She looks sort of familiar, but not until I get closer do I recognize her as Mrs. Sandoval.

"... I was able to find a sitter for her brother, but I know she'd hate to miss the dance, so if it's really not too much trouble..."

No way. Miss Independent needs a ride?

Papi shakes his head. "It's no trouble. I'll take the girls to the dance and bring them home afterward. You can pick Julia up in the morning."

Mrs. Sandoval thanks him and finally notices me. "Stef, we've missed you!" she says, stepping back as if she's admiring a painting. She checks her watch. "Ooh. I better get back to work. You girls have a great time at the dance. I'm so proud of all the work you put in."

After she's out of earshot, I remind Papi that I'm not going to the dance.

"You don't have to go," he says, "but it looks like we're taking Julia."

Neither of us knows quite what to do next. Do I go back and get her? Do we honk? Luckily, Mrs. Sandoval has thought of that. I pick her out of the crowd that's still milling in front of our school building. She straightens Julia's cardigan and looks like she's explaining something to her. All of a sudden, Julia jerks away and scowls. Mrs. Sandoval throws up her arms and starts walking back toward Tía Perla. A few seconds later, Julia throws back her head and follows.

When they get to the truck, Mrs. Sandoval gives Papi a you-know-how-they-are smile. Then she kisses Julia on the forehead and practically shoves her inside. "Have *fun*. Be po*lite*." Julia slams the door. She senses me trying to catch her eye and looks away, studying her fingernails like she just realized they're diamond-encrusted.

None of us says a word on the ride home. Once, at a red light, Papi starts tapping nervously on the steering wheel until I nudge him to quit. We can't be sure what might set her off.

Back at our house, Papi unlocks the front door, and Julia stalks off for my bedroom like it hasn't been forever since the last time she visited. Papi and I shrug at each other, then I follow Julia down the hallway. I find her sprawled on my bed. She puts her hands over her face and stops me before I can say anything. "Don't even."

I do anyway. "Why don't you just take the bus?"

She sits up. "Right? I've been riding the bus all year, and it's like they *still* don't trust me. I have to *text* when I get on, *text* when I get off, and if I'm even *two* minutes late, it's, like, call the FBI or something."

"So, *we're* taking you to the dance?"

"I guess."

"And you're not worried about smelling like tacos?"

Julia opens her mouth but changes her mind and flops back down on my bed. "I don't know why I say things like that. Maddie thought I was . . . cool, or whatever. And . . . I don't know. Sorry. Anyway, *you're* the one who ditched me for Amanda!"

Now I'm the one who opens my mouth, about to lob back an argument, until I realize it's kind of true. I never thought of it that way before, but the more time I spent with Amanda, the less I spent with Julia—even before Julia started taking the bus to school. It wasn't on purpose. Amanda and I just had more in common, I guess. Had more fun together.

"Sorry, too." I slide to the floor, my back against the wall, and sit there until Julia breaks the awkward silence by hopping off my bed and tearing through my wardrobe.

"Make yourself at home," I say, getting up to stop her, though I quickly see there's no point trying.

"Well, it's not like my genius mother thought to pack me any extra clothes," she answers from inside my closet, her voice muffled by my sweaters and dresses. "And I'm not going in my *uniform* obviously. What are you gonna wear?"

I tell her I'm not going to the dance. We can give her a ride, but I'm not going.

"Don't be dumb," she says. "Here." A black button-up sweater flies at my face. As soon as I manage to swat it away, a plum-colored skirt hits me.

"Hey!"

"Just put it on."

I sigh and start changing. It's easier than fighting with her. A few minutes later, Julia emerges from behind my closet door in a flowery pink sundress and jean jacket, sleeves rolled up to her elbows. The outfit looks like she's been planning it for weeks, but at the same time, effortless. So annoying. "At least you don't have completely terrible taste," she says.

"Are you always this charming when you steal people's clothes?"

She shrugs and smiles, sparkling-sweet as ever. "Now," she orders. "Sit."

I let Julia bully me into the chair at my desk, but not even she is bossy enough to force my curls to behave, I think. Nonetheless, she twists and pulls and yanks and spritzes and, somehow, it works. Mami would be thrilled.

CHAPTER
33

We ride to school in Tía Perla, me squished between Papi and Julia on the bench seat. When we get there, Papi tells Julia he'll be back in a couple of hours and to call if she needs anything. "See you," I say.

Julia whips her head back around. "Come *on*. We're already late. I'm not walking in there by myself." She grabs my wrist and tugs.

"No, I told you. I'm not going." I tug my arm back and plant myself squarely in the middle of the seat.

"Stef, *seriously*, just come with me?" She's really asking me to go with her, and not just trying to boss me around. Deciding I might as well check on Arthur and see how Amanda's decorations turned out, I slide out the door and tell Papi I'll be right back.

I expect to hear music as we get closer to the gym. Instead, what we hear are two boys—I don't recognize them from Saint Scholastica—on their way back to the parking lot.

"Just have your mom come get us now. No Viviana *and* no dance?"

Julia and I look at each other and start walking faster.

Outside the gym, students are shuffling around looking bored and disappointed. The teachers who came to chaperone are huddled up, shaking their heads and shrugging their shoulders. A few parents linger nearby, glancing at their watches. Mr. Salazar is pacing the breezeway, a phone held up to one ear and a hand pressed against the other.

I spot Arthur, and he walks right over, pulling his headphones down around his neck. "I thought you weren't coming."

"I'm not. What's going on?"

"Power went out in the gym. Mr. Salazar is trying to get it fixed, but the ice cream already melted and the sodas are all warm. No lights, no speakers, no music."

That means no dance. The teachers have started refunding everyone's admission.

And that means no art supplies, I think.

"What *happened*?" Julia asks.

"The DJ," Arthur says. "Tripped a circuit breaker when he was setting up."

Julia screams into her hands. "No, no, no, no, *no!*" She pulls out her cell phone and frantically dials. When her mom doesn't pick up, she screams again and storms off. I don't blame her. This dance is a disaster, and it's our fault. Part of me wants to follow Julia, to crawl under my bed and hide forever. But part of me knows we can't just leave this mess behind us. So I close my eyes and think. Hard. From the gut.

And then I have it.

I tell Arthur to find Amanda and meet me back in the parking lot. Then I chase after Julia and grab her by the elbow. She whips around. "Let's just *go.*"

"No," I tell her. "Tía Perla!"

"Tía *what?*" But then, as she starts to understand, the lights in her smile begin to flicker back on.

"I'll go talk to my dad—you tell everyone the dance is moving."

Papi is humming to himself with one arm draped out the window when I get to the truck. I throw open the door, and he starts to turn the key. "Ready to go? Shall we take Tía Perla out for a couple of hours until it's time to pick up Julia?"

"No, wait." Panting, I try to explain the dance debacle as quickly as I can. "Can we fire up Tía Perla, like, right here?"

He starts nodding, slowly at first and then eagerly. "Órale!" he growls. This time it means "YES!" Then he slaps his palm on the steering wheel so hard the horn blares—as if Tía Perla herself is whooping in excitement. "Órale!"

CHAPTER
34

Arthur and Amanda come rushing to the parking lot as Papi hooks up Tía Perla's generator and I lift open her canopy. Amanda finds a take-out bag in the kitchen, writes DONATIONS on one side in black marker, and sets it on the card table. Arthur pulls an armful of sodas from the ice chest and starts passing them around to the students and parents and teachers who followed Julia out here but still aren't sure what's going on. I scramble back into the cab, crank down the windows, and turn up Papi's radio. He has it tuned to banda again. No, thanks. I twist the dial and, like magic, find Viviana Vega.

I sink down into the bench seat to catch my breath and enjoy the moment.

Arthur interrupts. "Hey, turn it back!" he hollers from outside.

I poke my head out the window.

"What?"

Arthur, Amanda, and Julia yell back at me in unison: "Turn it back!"

Oh well, I think. Órale!

The joyful, driving rhythm of Papi's music begins to break up the clumps of middle schoolers standing around Tía Perla. A flourish of horns set Julia and Amanda swaying, shoulder to shoulder, *oompah-pah, oompah-pah*. Jangling guitar chords relax the worried lines on Mr. Salazar's forehead until he's clinking soda bottles with the other teachers. Students tap their feet as they wait in line for the nachos, quesadillas, tortas, and—for Arthur—the wheat-free, dairy-free, egg-free, nut-free, meat-free specialty-of-the-house super burrito that Papi and I slide through the window as fast as we can.

I'm dusting cilantro over the top of two street tacos when Papi stops me. "I can handle this, m'ija. You should be out there." I look doubtfully at the line outside the truck.

"Really," he urges. "Go." Then he hands me a tortilla, fresh off the grill and smeared with butter. I take a big bite—it's as warm and familiar as home—then leave the tortilla on the counter while I look for Arthur and Amanda in the crowd.

They're selling Amanda's origami stars, fifty cents apiece. Students are swinging them over their heads like lassos, the metallic wrapping paper winking under the parking lights. I take both their hands and pull them closer to Tía Perla, where the music is loudest. I twirl Arthur under one of my arms and Amanda under the other. Then they close the circle, and we spin until we fall over laughing.

It seems like only minutes before the first parents start arriving for pickup. Tía Perla's kitchen is nearly empty, but the donation bag is full—so full that a few crumpled-up bills have fallen to the ground. Julia and I pick them up and stuff them inside the bag before presenting it to Mr. Salazar.

He tries to give some of the money back to Papi. But Papi just folds his arms over his chest, shakes his head, and smiles.

"Do you think it's enough?" I ask.

Mr. Salazar looks like he can't quite believe it. "I'd say so." He nods. "More than enough."

When everything is cleaned up, Papi hands Julia and me a strawberry soda each. "Saved these for you." We climb back into the cab, crank the radio up as loud as it will go, and sing all the way back home. I don't even care who sees us.

CHAPTER
35

Julia and I are still up chattering in my bedroom when Mami comes home from her shift at the grocery store.

She taps on my door before nudging it open. "Girls? It's very late. I heard you had an exciting night, but if you can't get to sleep, at least keep your voices down. Papi has to be up early tomorrow. Someone is coming over to check out the truck."

So soon? I deflate.

Lying on the floor with our feet propped on my bed, Julia and I reminisce about afternoons on my front porch and about Tía Perla.

"Why does he have to sell her anyway?" Julia yawns. "I mean, she's not *that* bad."

She *isn't* that bad. Not bad at all. And maybe he doesn't have to sell her.

"Get up." I elbow Julia as I spring to my feet.

"What for?" she moans. "It's so late. You heard your mom."

I'm already tearing through my stash of art supplies. I'm going to come through for Tía Perla like she came through for me.

"Just get up. And put your shoes back on. And don't make a sound."

It's colder in the driveway than I thought it would be, but with our extra-bright porch light, it's at least bright enough to see. Shivering, I squirt globs of red and white paint onto a paper plate. I hand it to Julia with a paintbrush, showing her how to touch up the flaking roses on Tía Perla's side. While she works, I add swirling blue clouds and curling green vines—the same as in the drawing I made the day of the Viviana Vega concert. Only now I don't want Tía Perla to fly out of our lives after all. Instead, I imagine her soaring into a newer, brighter future, with all of us inside.

I carry chairs out from the kitchen, and Julia and I stand on them to reach the high spots. When we're done, we step back on the grass to examine our work.

"Looks good," Julia says finally. "Only, I never understood the name. I mean, do you even have an Aunt Pearl?"

She's right. This truck isn't just crazy, old Tía Perla—she's so much more.

"I'm not quite finished here," I tell Julia. "But you can go back inside." As she tiptoes up the front steps, I squirt two more puddles of paint onto a fresh paper plate.

CHAPTER
36

Julia is snoring on my bedroom floor when the alarm clock starts bleating. I want to pull the covers back over my head and snore along with her, but then I remember Papi's appointment. I get out of bed, step over Julia, and race to the kitchen.

Mami and Papi are at the table, sipping their coffee.

"Estefania," Mami says, "I wasn't expecting you up for hours. When did you two finally get to bed?"

I wave off her questions. "Has that man come? About the truck?"

"He'll be here soon," Papi says. "I was about to go out and wipe down the counters."

Not too late, then. "Good." I look from one of my parents

to the other. "I need you to come outside with me. Both of you. Now. Please."

"Estefania?" Papi asks.

"M'ija," Mami says, looking down at her bathrobe. "I'm not even dressed."

"Please, just come."

I dart ahead, open the front door, then spread my arms across it to hold them back. "Okay. Don't be mad. Just think about it." Then I step aside and sweep my arms toward the driveway, introducing them to:

THE TACO QUEEN.

She looks even better than she did in the moonlight. Not perfect—still dented, but not so dull. Tired, maybe, but full of life and promise.

A laugh catches in Mami's throat as soon as she sees it, and she wipes a tear off her cheek. Papi comes closer. "M'ija... how... I don't..." he starts and stops.

"I'm not ready to give her up," I say, making up a new speech, there on the lawn. This time, instead of the mayor holding a gavel, I'm facing Papi, who's holding his breath. "I know how nice those other trucks look, but if I could do this overnight with Julia, just think what we could all do. Together. And anyway, it's like I said: Tía Perla isn't really my aunt. But she is like family."

Papi runs his finger over the freshly painted letters, black outlined in gold. He doesn't say anything until we all hear a car slow to a stop in front of our house. As the man opens his door, Papi startles and walks out to the end of the driveway, stopping between the man and Tía Perla.

"Is this the—" the man starts to say.

"No," Papi interrupts. "It was a mistake. I'm very sorry, but she's not for sale after all."

The man turns to Mami, who smiles and shakes her head. Then he gets back into his car and drives away.

When he disappears, I run to Papi and jump onto his back. He catches me under my knees and laughs his biggest, thundering laugh.

"Órale!" I shout, looking up at the sky and then at the miles and miles of road just waiting for us. "Órale!"

Acknowledgments

To my family back home and in Stockton; to the first-generation families who trusted me with their stories during my years at the *Record*; to my agent, Jennifer Laughran; to my editor, Nikki Garcia, and the Little, Brown team; and to David, Alice, and Soledad: I am so grateful.

Jennifer Torres is the author of *Stef Soto, Taco Queen*; *Flor and Miranda Steal the Show*; and *Finding the Music/En pos de la música*. She lives with her family in Southern California.